SITUATIONAL SELLING

SITUATIONAL SELLING

Six Keys to Mastering the Complex Business Sale

Paul J. Kelly

American Management Association

This book is available at a special
discount when ordered in bulk quantities.
For information, contact Special Sales Department,
AMACOM, a division of American Management Association,
135 West 50th Street, New York, NY 10020.

Library of Congress Cataloging-in-Publication Data

Kelly, Paul J.
  Situational selling.

  Includes index.
  1. Selling. 2. Sales personnel. I. Title.
HF5438.25.K46 1988   658.8'5   87-47844
ISBN 0-8144-5938-2

Printing number

10 9 8 7 6 5 4 3 2 1

Contents

INTRODUCTION: WHAT THIS BOOK CAN DO FOR YOU

Have you ever struggled to gain a customer's attention to the really important differences between your product and a competitor's? Are you concerned with the proliferation of high-quality "me too" products coming into your market? Have you experienced the frustration of trying to motivate a customer to change the way he does business? Or become angry when your own people seem unappreciative of the effort an effective sales campaign requires?

You're not alone. In business after business a formidable combination of technological advances, foreign competitors, changing buying attitudes, and increasingly complex products have radically changed the roles and fundamental responsibilities of the sales representative.

Issues like these and others have become the battleground of the modern salesperson. Unlike your predecessor of 20 years ago, whose major mission was to convince buyers of the value and benefit of his product, you must contend with a new agenda—an agenda that demands that you as the salesperson become a part of the "package" offered, by offering value-added services and advice from seasoned, knowledgeable salespeople.

If one thing has become clear to me after training and consulting with over 300 leading American companies it is this: selling in the business-to-business arena requires considerably more skill, knowledge, and capability than simply knowing what your product or service can do.

The Business-to-Business Arena

Indeed, while knowledge of your product is important it's also *expected*. Do you for a moment think that your competitors don't know their product? That they somehow became formidable competitors by luck? No. They not only *know* their product as well as you do, chances are they also *have* the products to do the job. Thinking they don't is an arrogance that really won't survive in today's environment.

Your customer knows all about product. She has access to all the suppliers and, if she's smart, she's using that access to gain information, leverage purchasing power, and gain competitive advantage. What does she want that most salespeople can't or won't provide? Something new. She wants a *peer*, someone with whom she can confer and try out new ideas. She wants someone who knows so much about his product that his advice can be relied on and implemented without fear of failure or loss of status. She wants someone that will work with her to develop opportunities, someone whose goals are related to her own. Someone, in short, who puts *her* interests above his own. There are lots of people who can master the features, benefits, and applications of their product or service, but precious few that are willing to go that extra mile to really satisfy the customer's needs.

In many ways your role in the current marketing universe is closer to a Washington lobbyist than the product peddlers of yesterday. Like the lobbyist, a major part of your role is to create a favorable *climate* for your product. This doesn't necessarily involve coercion or even persuasion.

It's subtler than that. To excel you must assume new roles. Roles that were unheard of even ten years ago. A role is more than an act you put on for a customer: it's a commitment to a new way of selling. It may mean subordinating the desire for a quick order to protect a long-term relationship or sitting back and letting someone else sell because her skills are a closer match to what the customer wants. These roles may require walking away from a deal because the conditions just aren't right. Educator, negotiator, expert, strategist, conflict arbitrator, team leader, influencer, pioneer—the list goes on and on. This book was written to take stock of the new requirements put on you as a salesperson and to help you master them. After reading this book, you'll be able to:

- Gain total familiarity with your customers' objectives, strategies, operations, and culture.
- Constantly build a perception of product expertise with your customers by establishing yourself as a *resource* not simply a supplier.
- Differentiate *yourself* as well as your product by behaving in *unexpected* ways with your customers. When was the last time you really surprised a customer with a suggestion or piece of information?
- Leverage your relationship with the customer. Like Mario Puzo's Godfather, you can gain influence by developing a history of "favors" with the customer. Like the equity in your home, this history can be "borrowed" against at reasonable rates to make improvements to the basic relationship.
- Work with your own people in billing, claims, customer service, or any other area that interfaces with the customer to ensure that they too are aware of the requirements of today's market.

It's a big job, but it's the *only* job you've got. There are simply too many sales options available to your company to continue spending upward of $200 per sales call for a person who writes orders and handles an occasional complaint.

The Necessary Skills

You won't find tired old bromides about handling objections or 50 ways to close a sale. Those are the subjects of the old order.

Instead, you'll find a whole universe of analytical, planning, communication, and evaluation skills: skills that used to be the exclusive province of the "big ticket" high-powered sales executive assigned huge quotas and high-risk sales campaigns; skills that are now the province of even the most junior sales representative.

Skills like:

- Selling "concepts" to an account: proven ways to improve efficiency and productivity and reduce costs and human stress.
- Negotiating difficult issues like long-term pricing, terms, delivery, or returns arrangements.
- Gaining true corporate commitments to designate your company as a supplier of choice.
- Managing a business-to-business relationship by penetrating an account at various levels and satisfying needs at each level.
- Controlling the efforts of a sales team so that the customer gets one unified message from everyone with whom he deals.
- Opening new markets to your product through creative analysis, planning, and communication to a designated territory.

As you read this book, take time to review your own sales performance. Chances are, if you're successful, you're already doing some of the things suggested here. If you are, read the book with an eye toward providing a more systematic approach to your selling. If you're not, try to incorporate them as soon as you can.

As the march of marketing sophistication continues, the salesperson who can execute these roles may well be the *only* salesperson there is.

1

THE RULES
OF THE GAME

"A Good Salesman Can Sell Anything"

My first exposure to selling occurred when I was five. We had recently moved from New York City to the suburbs. On the third or fourth day in our new house the doorbell rang. When I opened the door a small, nervous man politely asked if my mother was at home. He introduced himself as Pete from Electrolux, the vacuum cleaner company. I think my mother was grateful for the company. She invited him in. They shared a cup of tea and began talking about his products. At first my mother was a little distant. She already owned a vacuum cleaner and her family had *always* used Hoovers. He worked relentlessly to persuade her to allow him to conduct a demonstration. I was fascinated. He hauled in the equipment, soiled the carpet, and talked incessantly about the product. I thought it was better than Howdy Doody. Every so often over the next few years, Pete would stop by. He sold us every attachment imaginable. Special tools for pet hairs (we didn't have a pet), extra long hoses for those "hard to get at places." You name it. He finally stopped coming: I guess because he had sold us everything he had to offer. My mother used to say she bought the stuff to get rid of him but I think it was more complicated than that.

In my view, Pete possessed some fundamental skills that every really effective salesperson has. First, of course, he knew his product. But more importantly, he understood the environmental issues connected with selling his product. He knew that a housewife, recently arrived from the city would be faced with four kids tracking in more mud than she ever thought existed. He sensed that a customer who had just moved into a new home would want the very best equipment and he quickly discovered that she had the necessary resources to get them. Beyond that he had the communication skills to keep her interested and in the right frame of mind for buying.

Two Selling Modes

With a few exceptions, most of today's selling can be classified into one of two categories or modes:

- The business-to-consumer mode
- The business-to-business mode

Much of the former mode is currently addressed through retailers and other channels such as catalogs or telephone marketing (although financial products like stocks and mutual funds and direct sellers like Avon, Amway, and Tupperware are notable exceptions). The business-to-business mode is also experiencing change but remains primarily a face-to-face sale in most cases.

To understand the different seller requirements in each mode, it might be helpful to examine the buyers briefly. After all, it's usually buyer behavior that largely determines successful seller behavior. If you can, take off your seller's hat for a moment and project yourself into the role of a buyer.

Buying Mazes

When making a purchase decision, whether in the business-to-consumer or business-to-business environment, most of us go through a series of smaller decisions or checkpoints before making the final buying decision. This "path to a decision" often seems like a maze to the seller. To me, one of the primary factors that separates successful sellers from their less successful counterparts is an ability to understand and capitalize on these mazes.

In the business-to-consumer maze, the buyers are relatively free. By that I mean they are not encumbered with a lot of organizational and market concerns. It's their money and they can do whatever they want with it. Because it's their money, they are very resource conscious, some searching endlessly for the best "deal." Many (though not all) are not always well informed, and they generally make their decisions on a very personal level. To the business-to-consumer seller the maze can be represented as in Figure 1-1.

Pete the Electrolux salesman was able to identify quickly some of my mother's *values*. Values have two components:

- Lifestyle, which includes attitudes, beliefs, opinions, hopes, fears, aspirations, and experiences.
- Needs, which include solutions to problems, functional capabilities (such as convenience or new applications), and personal satisfaction.

Once he had determined those issues, he had to ensure that the resources were available and that my mother was willing to part with them. In his case, it was a question of funds. In other sales, it may be credit worthiness.

Pete directed all his planning, communication, and follow-up skills at those issues. His function as a seller had four major components:

- To identify from the broad market of his territory those prospects who had values and resources that matched his product offering.
- To explore those values with the customer.

Figure 1-1

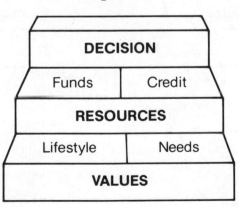

- To qualify buyers.
- To sell benefits.

Let's suppose, for a moment, that my mother was buying vacuum cleaners for a major corporation or institution. She's now being paid and evaluated on her buying decisions. She also has complete access to the corporation's information and purchasing power. Chances are she's made similar purchases before. In all likelihood she's going to be a lot more aggressive in seeking a better package of price and service extras. The maze for this decision might look like the one in Figure 1-2.

Pete's first task would be to position himself in the marketplace. Large organizations don't just buy from anyone. They require an "ante" or a price for playing the game. This level of the maze relates strongly to the product itself. Pete would have to demonstrate that his *pricing* was flexible and competitive with other suppliers. Indeed, he might have to answer a bid or other purchasing device. He would have to show a proven *track record* of success with other organizations with similar needs. *Information* from unbiased third parties or respected references would have to be provided as well as points of *difference*. Finally, my mother would have to be convinced that he could *distribute* and service

Figure 1-2

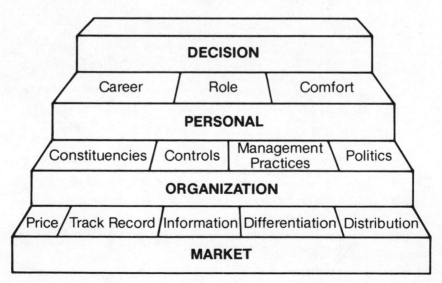

the machines at all her locations. The market level does not differ substantially from the business-to-consumer maze. A well-informed consumer might make many of the same demands.

Unfortunately for Pete, the selling doesn't stop there. Just because he has the best product at the best price and can support it across the organization doesn't mean he has the sale. Business organizations are a lot like countries. Actions are ruled at least as much by politics and appearances as they are by what's right for the organization. As a buyer, my mother would have to be concerned with all the *constituencies* that will be affected by the sale. The last thing she'd want is a lot of complaints from the maintenance departments or a memo from a Vice President saying the carpets don't seem as clean as they once were. She'd want assurances that everyone will be absolutely satisfied with the product. She'd have to be very aware of the *controls* imposed on her by the organization. Spending more than the budget allows at home probably means a short conversation with my father and perhaps cutting back on a few nonessentials. At work, it means long explanations, perhaps a negative performance evaluation, and maybe even termination. She'd have to think long and hard about policies and guidelines pertaining to the purchase as well as any existing contracts that might be in place. She'd also be concerned with existing *management practices*. Does the company prefer that these decisions be made locally or centrally? What are the prevailing attitudes on inventory and backup equipment? Is leasing preferable to purchase? Finally, she'd have to consider the *political* ramifications. Did the chairman work for Hoover at one time? Does the head of maintenance have a vendetta against Electrolux? Is Regina a major customer?

Even after Pete addressed those issues, he wouldn't be finished. In the last level of the maze he'd have to address her personal concerns. She has a *career* to develop. Controversial or unpopular decisions don't make for promotions. Is the decision supportive of her *role* in the organization? If she's perceived as a technical expert, does this decision reinforce or damage that perception? If she's regarded as a ruthless cost cutter, how does Pete's pricing reflect that role? Finally, he'd have to address her personal *comfort* needs. Is she looking for recognition, promotion, or acceptance by the organization? Or does she want to maintain a low profile through safe, noncontroversial decisions?

Pete would have to direct his planning, communication, and follow-up skills at a whole different universe of concerns. His function as a business-to-business seller has three major components distinctly different from the business-to-consumer arena. He must:

- *Manage* change, relationships, and interfaces between his organization and the buying organization.
- *Develop* an awareness of problems and opportunities and detailed business cases to resolve or capitalize on them.
- *Lobby* with the various interest groups and power bases within the organization.

This is not to say that one selling mode is superior to or requires more professionalism than another. Both offer unique but markedly different challenges to the seller. Much has been written about improving selling on a business-to-consumer level but how do successful business-to-business sellers address their environment? Three examples may serve to demonstrate some of their approaches.

I recently traveled with a sales representative for a leading telecommunications company calling on telephone operating companies. We made a call on an engineer in the long-range planning department. The customer's responsibility was to develop plans for expansion or reduction of the telephone network in response to changes in the population within his operating area. The representative was familiar with the customer, though they were not apparently close.

The conversation quickly became highly technical, and I thought to myself: "Here we go, I'm about to get lost." And I did. To my surprise, however, the sales representative didn't seem to know a whole lot more than I did. As a technical question was asked, he would write it down almost verbatim and say: "I'll get technical services to give you that answer by next Tuesday" or "I'll have our customer service people provide that answer by the end of next week." By the end of the call, he had committed *other* people to provide more than a dozen answers within a three-week time frame.

"Is this selling?" I wondered. When I asked the sales representa-tive about this, he said simply: "Look, this guy wants answers, not bull. He knows I'm not as technically savvy as he is, so he uses me as a conduit to those that are. It doesn't hurt my feelings. My selling really starts now, when I try to get our own employees to get the information by these dates."

On another occasion, I traveled with a sales representative for a leading housewares company. We called on a major retailer who was having some problems with the line. We sat down, and the sales representative opened the call with a close. "Joe, I want you to take 30 dozen of our new product." The customer calmly punched three buttons on his desk-side terminal and said: "Fine, if you take back the 20 dozen of product X that I've been sitting on for the last six weeks."

What followed was a fascinating exchange of promises as well as some of the strongest "trust me" language I've ever heard. The representative promised to help the customer sell the excess inventory if he'd take the 30 dozen; they negotiated price, display strategies, merchandising ideas, and co-op advertising expenses. In the end, the customer took 25 dozen. When we left the rep said: "That's a pleasant surprise, I thought he'd only take 20 dozen." Not once did the conversation touch direct product benefits. It was a straight exchange of favors based on short-term personal interest, and it worked!

In a third case, I traveled with a computer time-sharing repre-sentative, calling on a department head of an established account that was not currently using the service. She started the call by saying that she had been referred by other department heads in the company. While she asked a few questions about the de-partment, the majority of the conversation was directed at the department head himself. Issues like where he had come from, how long he had been in the assignment, and even company gossip were discussed in depth. The rep closed the call with a request to conduct a study, to which the customer readily agreed. I would estimate that the total time dedicated to discussions of time-sharing was less than seven minutes.

When I congratulated the representative on her success, she explained: "That's the way things work in this company. They're very political and want to know what everybody else is up to. If everybody else is doing it, they'll do it. Now on our next call, I'll have to take an entirely different approach."

Each of these sales representatives was smart enough to see what the customer was looking for and respond accordingly. They increased customer ease and confidence by positioning themselves in the role the customer hoped they would assume instead of creating an image and *imposing* it on the customer. To me, this is the very essence of effective communication.

All of us have developed a certain wariness about other people. This is natural and is rooted in experience. Nowhere is this more evident than in business settings. Unfortunately, everyone we have met has not always treated us well. So we assume certain defense mechanisms in our dealings with others. We may not always be as open as we might like or as willing to understand the other side's point of view. Yet we secretly hope that the people we meet will live up to some more or less well-defined expectations that we have established. We'd like to be able to fit them into one of our mental cubbyholes. Certainly you can see this in love, friendship, and family. We can also add business-to-business selling environments because of the complexity of the selling maze.

It's this positioning oneself with customers that characterizes successful business-to-business selling. In order to capitalize on the business-to-business buying maze, the seller must become a *part* of the buying organization. She accomplishes this by assuming a *role* that matches or exceeds customer expectations. These roles communicate trust, reliability, expertise, and empathy. They neutralize the negative aspects of the maze and help move the decision through the business. What are these roles? That's the stuff of Chapter 2.

2

SIX ROLES THE SALES REPRESENTATIVE MAY ASSUME

If we accept that the successful sales representative achieves that success by the *role* he assumes in the account, it's important to determine what the possible roles are and then try to match the role to different situations.

The research for this book has included observations of over 5000 sales calls in every business-to-business arena. Salespeople for companies such as Pepsi-Cola, Miller Brewing, General Electric, AT&T, Sterling Drug, American Express, Avis Rent a Car, Pitney Bowes, and SONECOR Systems have all contributed to the results. In addition, numerous focus groups were held with all levels of sales and sales management in the industrial, commercial, retail, and service sectors. Finally, and perhaps most importantly, the insights and comments of the participants of over 200 sales and sales management seminars were recorded and analyzed.

While no two selling situations are exactly alike, it was possible to identify six possible roles that modern business-to-business sellers are assuming.

Two of the roles are *tactical*, that is, they have to do with the way the sales representative interacts on a face-to-face basis with the customer. The other four are *strategic*, in that they deal with the planning and controlling of the sales effort across extended time frames.

13

The two tactical roles are:

- The consultative seller
- The negotiator

These roles are determined by the product or service offered and the level of competition. The **consultative seller** is selling a product or service that the customer may not have thought about buying. These sellers *create* needs as well as satisfy them. Some examples might include new technology like voice mail, HMO medical plans, or consulting services to small businesses.

In the **negotiator** role, the customer has an ongoing need for the product or service but knows he can get equal or better quality from a number of vendors. Some examples might include food products, office supplies, and business forms.

The strategic roles are:

- The account affiliation manager
- The relationship manager
- The team seller
- The prospector

These roles are also determined by your product, but just as importantly by the level of decisionmaking within the purchasing organizations and by the concentration of accounts within your market.

In brief, the **account affiliation manager** works to gain a foothold in an environment where business-to-business affiliations are required. She is trying to gain the designation of "preferred vendor" or "exclusive supplier," where specifications must be met and implementation must take place across the account's operation. The **relationship manager** role is one where the sales representative calls predominantly on *existing* accounts with an eye toward increasing the share of the business within the account. The **prospector** role relates to those sales representatives who must cover a lot of ground and make many presentations in order to generate sales, and the **team seller** approach is used where internal "experts" such as technical or training support must be utilized in the selling effort.

Let's take a look at each of these roles, starting with the tactical roles—consultative seller and negotiator.

The Consultative Seller

Many organizations are attempting to position their salesforce as consultants to the customer base. These organizations are asking their sales representatives to establish themselves as experts in their field and confer with customers in solving problems and satisfying needs.

In many ways, the average sales representative should be well prepared for this role. He probably has had more training on the product than the customer. His day-to-day activities expose him to what other businesses are doing as well as to what competitive vendors are offering.

Sales representatives are often unequal to the task for a variety of reasons: they do not understand the underlying principles on which the customer's business operates, and many do not take the time or effort to discover what the customer's goals are. Successful consultative sellers have developed these skills, enabling them to position themselves as problem solvers in the account. In addition, a good consultative seller recognizes that a sale is a *change* and that most people approach change with an attitude of "if it ain't broke, don't fix it."

Much has been written about the resistance to change in today's organizations. Successful consultative salespeople have recognized that change is painful to the customer and have developed an approach that minimizes the pain by maximizing the customer's involvement in the change. How do they accomplish this? First, through a recognition that people will change only when they clearly and unmistakably see that the change is in their own best interest. Second, by taking it as an article of faith that this recognition comes from within each buyer and not as a result of being *told* by some outside party. Finally, by devising a strategy that *leads* the customer(s) through a thorough examination of their needs.

The Negotiator

Many sales representatives sell products that are readily available to the customer from a variety of sources. I hesitate to use the word "commodity" to describe these products or services because most sales representatives and marketing people would vehemently deny that they sell a commodity item. In fact, however, this is often how the customer views the product or service. Suffice it to say that the negotiator may be an appropriate role to take if three of the following five conditions exist:

- There are three or more approximately equal competitors for the business.
- No supplier controls more than 40% of the market.
- Customers are generally familiar with the product.
- Price promotion or discounting is common.
- The product is essential to conducting the customer's business.

Some examples of a situation where this might be an appropriate approach are national brand food products in the supermarket, airlines in the commercial market, or electrical supplies in the utilities market, all of which have heavy competition and limited differentiation.

When a sales representative recognizes that the need for his product or service exists and is ongoing, he should take the position of negotiator. Unlike the consultative seller, there is no doubt that the customer is going to buy: the question is from whom. Therefore, the negotiator does not spend a great deal of time relating the benefits of his product over the competition because this invariably leads to high-risk comparisons. Instead, he establishes positions that relate to interests on both sides. These interests may relate to cost, features, or services but may also relate to issues such as relationship, profit, growth, reliability, and responsiveness. The negotiator recognizes that a change of suppliers is fairly easily accomplished. He is therefore in a state of continual deal-making with his customers, rather than needs development or benefit selling.

Approaching the sale from the negotiator perspective requires several preconditions. First, the sales representative must have the authority (or at least quick access to the authority) to make adjustments to his positions. Second, the customer must be made aware that the sales representative has this authority so that he deals in good faith.

Sales negotiating differs from traditional negotiating (between, say, a union and management) for a few obvious reasons. On the surface, it appears that the customer is dealt a better hand in the sales negotiation. Where the union can shut down the plant, it is unlikely that the cola producer is going to deny a supermarket access to its products. While it's true that a supermarket *must* carry a national brand or face the wrath of its consumers, the *amount* it carries is largely at the discretion of the customer. Additionally, the customer may be conducting several negotiations at the same time and playing one supplier against another. This puts the sales representative at the mercy of competitors who may or may not be exercising good business judgment. Finally, the sales negotiator may not be able to rely on the support of his own management. Pricing decisions are generally not made solely by sales management, yet that is the only management to which most sales representatives have direct access.

Successful negotiators recognize these differences and address them when developing their approach. Specifically, they recognize that a buyer's interests may change from day to day or even hour to hour depending on the actions of the competition and the particular flow of business. They make it their business to determine these interests on *every* call and then tailor their proposals to those interests rather than some generic product benefit. Additionally, they know with certainty how far they can go in offering added value to the customer and develop a "settlement range" of alternative approaches should the buyer object. Unlike a traditional objection-handling process, these alternate approaches require the buyer to *give* every time he *takes*. This give and take continues along the settlement range. But parties define and defend their positions by providing rationales and principles to the other side. The negotiation is "won" when both parties come to a mutually agreeable settlement and each is satisfied that his or her needs are addressed.

While the consultative seller and negotiator tactics differ in their fundamental approach, there are similarities:

- They both concentrate on the customer rather than the product.
- They both require the sales representative to "lead" the customer through a thought process.

They are dissimilar in that:

- The outcome of the negotiator role is assured: the customer *will* buy a product or service. In the consultative role, there is no such assurance.
- The consultative seller positions the product as a solution, while the negotiator positions it as a benefit.
- The consultative seller takes a pro-active role in identifying problems, while the negotiator takes a reactive role to customer's stated goals.

In subsequent chapters, we review both roles in greater detail. For now, let's take a look at the strategic roles.

The Account Affiliation Manager

In the first strategic role—the account affiliation manager—the sales representative acts as an agent for developing a business-to-business affiliation between her company and the customer's company. This role is particularly relevant in business services, such as accounting services or travel services, but can be equally applicable to a broader range of products depending on the marketing strategies and programs of the producer. When successfully implemented, it usually results in an official designation like "preferred vendor" or "exclusive supplier."

The "sale" in this role is some sort of corporate or divisional directive that positions this designation and incorporates it in their official policies and procedures. Once that designation has been made, the rep may have to work to ensure the policy is implemented across the account's operations.

This affiliation is somewhat risky business for the buyers. Often their individual reputations are on the line and many are reluctant to make strong policy decisions. Many affiliations are subject to a sort of corporate inertia where initial interest is lost as the rep works through the organization. And, since agreements are more often than not just that—agreements, not contracts—commitments can be broken and the process must be started again.

Account affiliation managers are very strategically oriented. They recognize the political implications to the buyer and therefore develop a broad base of support at many levels of the organization. They're aware that an affiliation will be viewed from many different perspectives—profit, policy, performance, and others. They further accept that any one of these perspectives can "kill the deal" at any time during the process if their interests aren't met. They also plan their approach carefully and keep track of where they stand as the plan progresses.

The Relationship Manager

In this second strategic role, sales representatives are positioned against a specific set of *existing* customers where one or more suppliers share the business or where activity from competitive account affiliation managers is taking place.

These representatives assume a *defensive* as well as developmental role in the account. They are held accountable for increasing "share" within the account as well as providing intelligence and stalling competitive momentum. Three examples should make it clear just how relationship managers operate.

A leading medical imaging equipment manufacturer positioned its national account reps at the headquarters of major investor-owned hospitals (such as Humana and Hospital Corporation of America). These representatives had only one role—to establish and maintain a "presence" at corporate headquarters. Traditional "selling" was still carried out at the individual hospital level. The national account reps assisted in such duties as developing bids, providing technical seminars, developing budgets, and communicating guidelines to the individual hospitals.

A New Jersey-based packaged goods producer assigned a cadre of experienced representatives to the leading supermarket chains in the country. These representatives assisted in the development of chain-wide promotions and programs, merchandising, and point-of-sale materials. They worked to influence the plan-o-grams (the scheme by which the supermarket determines how much of which products it will display and where) with chain decisionmakers and helped implement programs with their own store-level sales reps.

A New York housewares producer positioned a select group of sales representatives against the major mass merchandisers (such as K-Mart and Walgreens). These highly experienced reps had two primary functions: to assist chain headquarters personnel in the development of new ways to sell the product at retail and to "intercept" small problems before they escalated. They spent as much time in accounts payable as they did in purchasing.

Normally, relationship managers will have more than a dozen

contacts within a single account. Some have as many as 50. The cast of customer characters often remains somewhat stable over time, so these representatives place heavy emphasis on developing a relationship with these individuals in order to strengthen their position. While the traditional vehicles of entertainment and gifts may be employed, they are not the primary means used by the successful relationship manager. More often, they formally identify influencers and decisionmakers within the account on a decision-by-decision basis. By that I mean they recognize that all decisions are not the same, and just because the treasurer made the decision the last time doesn't mean the office manager won't make it this time. They get to know their customers on more than one level. They want to know each buyer's perspective or how she views the business. They want to know how powerful she is and what sort of personality she has. Once they know this information, they try to run ideas "through the business" using different buyers as their "champions."

The Team Seller

Often the development of business and a clear explanation of product features and functions exceeds the capabilities of a single individual. Many sales require the addition of technical, customer service, customer education, or management support to reach desired goals. Technology sales come readily to mind in this situation. Often, mainframe computer or complex telecommunications sales require extensive marketing support from systems engineers and other technical experts. It's an equally appropriate approach, however, for certain business services where individuals will work on the project (such as advertising or management consulting) and the customer, client, or prospect wants to meet the entire team.

Sales representatives that assume the team seller role become responsible for the management of a sales campaign within the account. This generally requires quite a bit of strategy development prior to approaching the account, as well as forecasting the time and resource requirements. These campaigns will generally be executed over extended periods of time during which plans may change frequently owing to customer reactions.

The team seller's position is further complicated by the fact that in almost every team selling situation neither he nor his management has direct control over all the other members of the team. Systems engineers at IBM, for instance, often report to a systems engineering manager not to a sales manager. This is appropriate, since the range of skills required to carry out these jobs may employ skills well beyond the range of the sales manager. So the team seller is faced with the challenge of influencing a cadre of people whose skills he doesn't fully understand and whose cooperation cannot be counted on absolutely. This is often further complicated by major differences in style between the sales representative and the other team members as well as possible resentments between the team members. These resentments are often voiced in phrases such as "I do all the work and he gets all the glory." Clearly, the sales representative is faced with a major challenge in the team seller role.

Yet when it works well, there is no more effective sales strategy available. Successful team sellers are able to align their teams with people in the account who have similar concerns and interests. Engineers are able to have dialogues with other technical types, users with users, finance people with finance people. When this strategy is carried out well, the customer becomes almost overwhelmed with the effort and attention put forth; and, while objectives aren't always attained, *something* almost always happens. The trick, of course, is to make it work. Successful team sellers I have dealt with seem to work from similar sets of assumptions and plans. They recognize that *internal* selling is equally if not more important than external selling. Lining up the internal resources and "selling" them on the importance of a course of action has to be approached as seriously and professionally as getting the customer to agree to the course of action in the first place. They develop their plans in conjunction with the other team members. They do not deliver plans as a *fait accompli*. They solicit input and signoffs every step of the way. They seek opinions on appropriate time allocations for assigned tasks and generally instill enthusiasm throughout the team. They often defer to the "experts" and position themselves as a conduit of information, *not* as experts themselves.

The Prospector

The final role that the modern sales representative may assume is the prospector role. This role may be considered traditional, in that the sales representative is still positioned as the primary communicator of product or service capabilities.

This approach is often used in smaller organizations where the resources to conduct alternate sales channel strategies may not be available. But even in larger organizations, most salespeople still find the need to prospect from time to time.

In this role, sales representatives are expected to contact large numbers of customers and/or prospects across a territory. Often the product or service is relatively low in cost and risk to the buyer. Sales presentations are generally short, one- or two-shot deals where the prospector seeks an order on every call. Typically, the prospector will be required to close 20 or more orders per week and will be appraised on his ability to do so. Producers that opt for this strategy are relying on their salespeople to carry out more than just a sales function. They are requiring them to educate the customer, as well as handle complaints, provide public relations, and close sales. Often collection, delivery, and returns duties are also required of these representatives.

Organizations that assign this role to their sales representatives recognize that long-term relationships are not likely to increase overall sales significantly. They also recognize that their customer base or product line does not provide significant opportunity for developing further business opportunities within existing accounts. They have determined that their product has broad appeal within the marketplace and that the prospector is the logical means of tapping that appeal.

Primary examples of this role are local business machine dealers, retail services (such as credit cards or credit reports), traditional insurance salespeople, and food brokers. Many industries may also position a cadre of salespeople as new business development specialists to augment their other selling efforts with existing accounts.

Successful prospectors establish firm activity plans on a daily, weekly, and monthly basis. They recognize that they are involved to some extent in a "numbers game." The more *calls* they make, the more *sales* they'll make. They schedule their days carefully and route themselves through the territory in a strict "return on time invested" manner. Additionally, they target accounts to replenish their pool of prospects as well as to sign business on an ongoing basis. They concentrate heavily on qualifying accounts in terms of buying authority, availability of funds, and willingness to act quickly. They are able to maintain a high energy level and accept rejection well. No doubt, they build this attitude over the years, and it is typified by a remarkable ability to forget unpleasantness quickly and get on with the day's work.

Summary

From this brief explanation you can see that the traditional role of the sales representative as "peddler" has changed dramatically in the last 20 or 30 years. The increased burdens put on the sales representative have caused many organizations to revamp their traditional approaches to recruiting and selection, training, management, and control.

Many, if not most, organizations, however, have not gone far enough. The training curriculums of many of our finest corporations still limit the skill development activities of salespeople to simple communications skills directed at closing a sale on a single call. Management still attempts to measure *only* the results, rather than a combination of sales plan activities and results.

Much of what has been discussed in this chapter, however, can be done on an individual basis, through a combination of study and hard work. Which role is right for you? How do you really *master* these roles? These questions will be answered in subsequent chapters.

3

CHOOSING THE ROLE THAT'S RIGHT FOR YOU

If it's true that all salespeople are not created equal, how do you know which role is right for you? Normally, you'll be asked to assume only one of the tactical roles (sales negotiator or consultative seller). Market conditions may require, however, that you assume all four of the strategic roles (account affiliation manager, relationship manager, team seller, or prospector). Sorting out what conditions are influencing the roles you must assume is the purpose of this chapter.

I'm sure you've been able to see that my focus has been largely customer driven. I strongly believe that representatives must be responding to the customer base in everything they do. In order to determine which roles are right for you, a logical first step is to examine what your customers have come to expect in their dealings with salespeople like yourself. Let's start at the beginning.

How Market Conditions Determine Roles

Since the sales representative's environment is *the marketplace,* let's start determining roles by looking there.

You can analyze your market and how it influences the role you should take by considering four factors: the products or services you sell, the competition, the level of decisionmaking, and the concentration or relative numbers of accounts that have a major effect on your overall sales.

IIow Your Product or Service
Helps Determine Your Role

You should examine your product line from two perspectives:

1. Product maturity
2. Complexity (as perceived by *your* customer base)

It is a basic marketing principle that products and services go through a life cycle. When they are introduced, there is generally some wariness as the buyers become familiar with what it can provide them. As it matures, they become more comfortable with it, and (if it's worthwhile) its sales gain momentum. There comes a time, however, when the trend levels off and sales become flat. This is when the product is considered mature and further dramatic growth is considered unlikely. Companies typically start to promote their products aggressively at this point, so as to avoid erosion and sales decline.

Product Maturity

Why is the maturity of a product important in determining your role? It goes back to the hopes of the customer, which we explored earlier. None of us is really anxious to deal with the unknown. This is especially true in business where a wrong decision could tarnish our reputation. Most of us would rather stand pat and go with what we know. IBM's enormous success in the personal computer market has often been attributed to this phenomenon. Earlier products had just as many, if not more, capabilities but were avoided until "big blue" got into the fray. On the other hand, if we are totally familiar with a product, we begin to search for other reasons to buy. The designer jeans craze of a few years ago is an excellent example. When first introduced, they were sold exclusively in department stores and only at list price. As time passed, prices fell and people began to shop around. Now it's possible to find these jeans at many discounters, as well as flea markets and liquidators.

Products in the later stages of a life cycle are generally well known to customers. They have bought similar products in the past or have dealt with individuals who have. Often the product has been well publicized in both trade and mass market publications. The product has a proven track record that can readily be communicated by the sales representative through referrals, and price promotion has probably taken place. New products or products in the early stages of a cycle will typically require more explanation and demonstration. Additionally, customers will probably be more timid about making a purchase decision until a track record is established.

This gives us our first clue to which *tactical* role you should assume. If your products are in the early stages of the life cycle, a consultative approach may be required, while older products would probably lend themselves to the negotiator approach.

Life cycles vary by product line and market, and it's difficult to define where your product may stand from a generic point of view. However, answering the following statements may give you some direction in determining your product or service maturity level:

1. Most of my customers have bought my product or similar competitive products before.   T   F

2. Most customers *do not* consider it risky to buy my product.   T   F

3. My product is promoted often (i.e., discounts, special deals, or other incentives are offered).   T   F

4. Unit sales (not dollar) of my product generally increase less than 10% per year.   T   F

5. There are more than three competitors offering similar products to my customers.   T   F

6. The majority of my customers deal with more than one supplier in purchasing this product.   T   F

7. My company can count on *repeat* sales to produce more than 70% of *total* sales.   T   F

0. The majority of objections I hear relate to   [T] [F]
    price.

9. In most cases customers will buy products   [T] [F]
    like mine from the supplier who offers the
    lowest price.

10. It is very difficult for most buyers to see the   [T] [F]
    difference between my products and the
    competition's.

If you answered true to six or more of these questions, you can probably assume that your product is at least heading for a high maturity level—if it's not already there.

Just because a product is mature, don't make the mistake of thinking it's dull or unchallenging. On the contrary, in my view, sales expertise is really displayed when the product must be differentiated by the sales representative.

Product Complexity

Product complexity is an important consideration because it too affects customer behavior.

Let's consider two products—a refrigerator and a personal computer. Would you approach the two purchases in the same way?

When purchasing the computer, you may be concerned with issues like price, memory, and speed. But if you're like me, your initial concern will be: "How do I use it?" You'd want to understand it before you buy it, so you'll seek a dealer who will help you during and after the sale.

On the other hand, when shopping for a refrigerator, you'd consider yourself an expert on how to *use* the refrigerator. So you'd shop around, hit the discounters, and buy from the dealer who gave you the best deal, even if the salesperson knew nothing about refrigerators. After all, a "refrigerator is a refrigerator."

This demonstrates that complexity is an issue in determining your role, but also that complexity is, to some extent, in the eye of the beholder. The more the buyer knows about a product, the more the salesperson can focus on the product itself (e.g., its feature, price, differences) and the less he needs to focus on product application and customer education.

Complexity *is* an important issue, for a number of reasons:

1. It will often determine the level of decisionmaking in the account.
2. It will determine the level of risk for the buyers.
3. It may determine how the product or service is paid for.
4. It may dictate that others become involved in the sale.

A product that customers find difficult to understand will probably increase their timidity, resulting in elevation of the decisionmaking process as middle managers seek to "share the blame" and explore how the whole company can use it. Once a decision is elevated, the benefit story must change. Typically, middle managers are concerned with operation issues like price, delivery, or service. Senior management concerns itself more with strategies or corporate issues like growth, productivity, or image.

Many companies are not adequately funded in operating or capital budgets to purchase products they don't fully understand. This may require the development of a complex business case for presentation to senior management for the release of discretionary funds. This business case may require an analysis of the current situation, a statement of goals, recommendations for action, and a cost/benefit justification.

Less complex products, on the other hand, may be viewed almost as commodities. While the need for these products may be ongoing, the choice of suppliers may be wide. This allows the customer to take a more aggressive approach. How much more risk, for example, does the traffic manager take in leasing Fords rather than Chevrolets? Or the purchasing manager in buying one business form over another? These less complex products are often included in operating or capital budgets based on historical data. Price becomes a primary issue as does delivery and service.

An analysis of product complexity leads us to a decision on tactical roles. Because of the need to explore current needs and possible applications, the complex product would seem to lend itself to the consultative approach, while the less complex products might lend themselves more to the negotiator approach.

Complexity is a very individual subject. It requires that you have a firm understanding of your customer and your products or services. Answering the following statements may help you analyze your situation:

1. Most of my customers have never bought a product like mine before. T F

2. Most of my customers *do not* have a firmly established budget for my product. T F

3. The decision to buy my product is usually made by senior executives (VP or above). T F

4. It's nearly impossible to sell my product without support from technical or performance experts. T F

5. Most customers have to be *educated* on my product before they'll consider buying it. T F

6. Most middle managers consider it risky to buy a product like mine. T F

7. Most people who have bought my product in the past have required some cost/benefit justification in writing. T F

8. More than 50% of my sales are to first-time buyers of this type of product. T F

9. The major benefits of my product are business related rather than product related. For example, it contributes to productivity rather than being the least expensive. T F

10. The purchase of my product almost always requires more than one approval. T F

If you answered true to six or more of these statements, you probably have a product with a fairly high level of complexity.

Complex products and services are not necessarily more difficult

to sell. They simply require a different approach. Because of the
risk involved and the complexity of the decisionmaking process, it's
likely that complex products will also be high-ticket products and
that specific account strategies will be in place. Time frames on
decisions may be longer and a sales representative will be an
integral part of that decision. However, because the product's
complexity is so great, the level of traditional selling required may
be quite low. Consultative skills and an ability to *answer* questions
may be more important than persuasion skills and an ability to *ask*
questions.

Complexity may also determine one of the strategic roles. As
stated earlier, high-technology products and sophisticated business
services (like advertising or consulting) often require a team seller
approach. In part, this will depend on the resources that your
organization supplies. But it's a pretty safe bet that complex products will require some sort of team selling while simple products
will not.

Competitive Factors in Determining Your Role

As you well know, in nearly all selling arenas the competition
can determine what role you take in a sale—almost as much as you
can. Irresponsible pricing or sales strategies by one competitor
may affect an entire industry for many years. This has been clearly
demonstrated in such major industries as steel, casualty insurance,
and airlines. Producers faced with competitive pressures often
have no choice but to respond. This, in turn, puts pressure on the
bottom line and increases the need for quick sales to cover losses or
profit declines. Sales representatives get caught in the middle and
are often not able to perform their jobs the way they'd like.

Market share will often have a major influence on how customers
buy and thus how reps sell. Companies with shares in excess of
50% in a given product line can often afford to take a firm stand on
issues like pricing and service enhancements, while smaller shares
will usually dictate a more flexible approach.

Products where no single supplier controls more than 25% of the
market are generally considered commodity items, and buyers will
likely want to negotiate. The quality of the competition will also
have a major effect. If the offerings are comparable in quality and
function, the sales representative will have to address the competi-

tion regularly through demonstrations and business case comparisons. Price will again become a major determining factor in the sale. In situations where price, quality, and function are similar and market share is more or less evenly distributed among two or more suppliers, customers will often seek to develop a relationship with one supplier and direct all or a major portion of their business in that direction, in order to reduce the amount of time they spend with sales reps.

Where levels of competition are low, a consultative approach may be called for tactically and a prospector approach strategically. In highly competitive environments, the negotiator is the best tactic while the relationship manager and account affiliation manager approaches would be appropriate strategically. Team selling may be appropriate in either case.

Your level of competition might seem fairly obvious to you, but you may want to answer the following statements to get a clear picture:

1. No supplier controls more than 25% of my market.

2. There are at least three competitors that offer products more or less equal to mine in price, feature, or functions.

3. My product is often promoted (i.e., discounts or special deals are common).

4. It is very difficult to get customers to understand the difference between my product and the competition's.

5. Many of my customers play one competitor against another.

6. Most of my customers buy from one or more of my competitors, as well as from me.

7. Most of my customers buy on price more than anything else.

8. It's relatively easy for a customer to switch   ☐T ☐F
   from one vendor to another.

9. Most of my customers are *not* loyal to any   ☐T ☐F
   one supplier.

10. I regularly lose sales because a competitor   ☐T ☐F
   matches my offer.

If you answered true to six or more of these statements, the odds are that you conduct business in a highly competitive environment. The role you assume in this environment depends to a large degree on the position you hold in the marketplace.

Level of Decisionmaking and Your Role

Our third area of inquiry in determining which sales role is right for you is the level of decisionmaking within the account. As I stated earlier, the concerns of senior management are often not the same as those of middle managers or first-line supervisors. Because of this disparity, you may have to assume a different role with one group than you do with the others.

Senior managers of any operation, regardless of size, are accountable for the operation on a very broad range of business issues. They must first and foremost ensure acceptable levels of profitability on an ongoing basis. They must demonstrate and maintain a growth pattern acceptable to their stockholders or other investors. They are vitally concerned with remaining competitive and focus their attention on reducing costs through enhanced productivity and increased volume. But beyond that, their behavior and business practices vary greatly.

Senior managers make their livings by making decisions. They spend almost all their time at meetings where they are presented with facts and figures and asked to commit resources to projects and proposals. As a result, they have employed certain tools that they hope will help them get to the heart of the matter. One of these is the business case. This is a document that concisely explains the problem, the recommended solution, and cost justification. Subordinates are expected to make their proposals in this "format" so that reviews can be expedited and approvals granted. A stratagem that senior managers often employ is assuming a demeanor that tells very little about what they're thinking. This "poker face" reaction is really a defense mechanism. Think about it. If your main job was to listen to people pitch you for money or other resources, wouldn't you try to hide enthusiasm and disappointment? The last thing you'd want is to be pegged as a "mark" by your subordinates.

Middle managers, on the other hand, take an entirely different approach. They too make decisions on a daily basis, but few have been able to have the luxury of requiring a standardized process for presenting the problem. They must react quickly to the everyday fires with which every business is faced. As a result, they are likely to be more open about their needs and requirements. These needs are generally less global than the senior managers and relate to issues such as remaining within budget, ensuring prompt and reliable delivery, and keeping the users happy.

I'm not proposing that *every* senior manager will be reserved and analytical or that every middle manager will be open and concise in expressing business needs. A company founder, for example, may still be very involved in the day-to-day operations and take a firefighter approach, while a middle manager on the fast track, trying to impress her senior management, may take on the behavior of those managers. Yet, in trying to determine what role you should assume in the sale, it's a pretty safe bet that most of the people you meet will fit into these admittedly stereotypical profiles.

So, if your product or service is purchased by senior managers or requires senior management approval, the consultative and relationship manager approaches would be appropriate. If your product is purchased by middle managers or users, the negotiator approach may be appropriate. The relationship manager, account affiliation manager, or prospector approaches will depend on the concentration of your accounts, while the team seller approach depends to a large extent on the nature of your product or service.

It's easy to confuse titles with authority. I have encountered individuals with middle manager titles who had quite a bit of buying authority, while some vice presidents can't do anything without seeking permission. Why not answer the following statements to profile the level of decisionmakers in your territory:

1. The majority of my customers are more interested in how my product will contribute to the growth of the company than in issues like price or delivery.

2. Most of my customers demand that I show in writing how my product or service will help them either reduce costs or contribute to growth.

3. The majority of my sales require a formal presentation at some point in the sales cycle.   [T] [F]

4. My product or service is generally *not* paid for from operating or capital budgets.   [T] [F]

5. My sale requires a written proposal to get the business.

6. Many of my customers *do not* display emotion easily.   [T] [F]

7. Most of the time, customers must obtain more than one approval before buying my product or service.   [T] [F]

8. My product is perceived as a risky purchase by most of my customers.   [T] [F]

9. My product requires that customers allocate resources other than money (such as people) to make the purchase work for them.   [T] [F]

10. The purchasing department is generally *not* able to make the decision on buying my product or service.   [T] [F]

If you answered true to six or more of these statements, you probably have a fairly high level of decisionmaking in your market. If you accept that the environment determines or at least affects the way in which you do business, then this factor of the environment may have the greatest effect of all.

Market Concentration and Your Role

The final consideration in determining your role in the sales process is market concentration. Increasingly, sales management is redeploying its salesforces to call on only major accounts, those who are perceived to have the greatest potential for growth. Smaller accounts are in many cases being serviced by alternate sales channels, such as dealers or telemarketing. These redeployments have radically changed the way many sales representatives spend their time. Most salespeople are familiar with the 80-20 rule, which states that 80% of your sales will come from 20% of your accounts. Many organizations now conduct their face-to-face sales on that basis.

The concentration of accounts in your territory is important because it more or less determines *where* you will spend your time as well as the activities you will have to perform in the accounts.

It is very difficult for me to define what constitutes high concentration in *your* territory. Factors such as the length of the sales cycle, seasonal nature of your business, and service requirements would all have a bearing on whether or not you can consider yourself to have a high or low concentration of accounts. However, it has been my experience that reps who have less than a dozen major accounts (18 in urban areas owing to decreased travel requirements) are often able to provide the close scrutiny needed to carry out many of the major account strategies we have been discussing, as well as develop new business and service existing accounts. I would therefore estimate that if 12 accounts or less produce more than 70% of your business (18 accounts in urban areas), you can consider your territory highly concentrated. If you have more than 16 accounts (22 in urban areas) producing 70%, consider your territory lightly concentrated.

Now these formulas are not hard and fast. If your sales cycle is very short (say two or three calls to make a close), you might be able to expand this by 20% or so.

In markets where the concentration is high, the strategic approaches of account affiliation manager and relationship manager are appropriate. This is because of the high stakes at risk in every one of these select accounts. Careful planning of a sales campaign is critical to avoiding careless mistakes that could cost dearly.

In markets where the concentration is low the prospector

approach is appropriate because of lower risk factors and a broader distribution of opportunity.

The negotiator, team seller, and consultative seller approaches are largely unaffected by the market concentration.

Summary

Let's try to put this information together by reviewing what you've read so far. You'll recall that the role you assume can be defined somewhat by conditions that exist in the marketplace. This is because many experts feel that behavior is determined or at least influenced by our environment, and the environment of the sales representative is the marketplace. I've presented this environment from four perspectives: product, competition, level of decisionmaking, and market concentration. I hope that you have been able to determine where you stand in relation to these four

Table 3-1

	High		Low	
	Tactic	**Strategy**	**Tactic**	**Strategy**
Product maturity	Negotiate	—	Consult	—
Product complexity	Consult	Team Sell	Negotiate	—
Level of competition	Negotiate	Relationship Account Affiliation	Consult	Prospect
Level of decisionmaking	Consult	—	Negotiate	—
Market concentration	—	Relationship Account Affiliation	—	Prospect

areas. Are you high or low in the product maturity area? Do your customers find your product highly complex or relatively easy to understand? Are you selling to the highest echelons of the corporation or to middle managers and users? And finally, are you getting the majority of your business from a few accounts or from a broad spectrum? The true/false exercises should give you an indication. Use Table 3-1 to pinpoint which roles you should assume.

The remainder of this book is divided into detailed explanations of how to carry out these roles in your day-to-day selling. You may choose to read them all or only those that apply to you.

4

THE CONSULTATIVE SELLER

When a Sale Is Consultative

The consultative seller is a tactical role; that is, it relates to the face-to-face encounter between the sales representative and the customer(s).

A salesperson can be called consultative when the outcome of the sale is not assured prior to the initial contact. Now you may say to yourself: "I've been selling for years and believe me the outcome is never known." I'd agree with that statement up to a point. The outcome—the specific vendor, number of units, price, or delivery—is seldom known but *an* outcome is *assured*. General Motors *is* going to buy steel; United Airlines is a safe bet to buy fuel. Business, medicine, government, and education all need a steady flow of goods and services to operate. They have established budgets, policies, and procedures to ensure that purchases are made efficiently. The vendor who gets the business, the price the buyer pays, and the features received are all in doubt—but in the end a purchase *will* be made.

Contrast this with the situation the consultative seller faces. This sales representative must venture into territory where customers may not know they have needs, where solutions may not be totally understood, and motivation to change may be totally lacking. In the consultative environment, budgets have not been established, procedures are not in place, and the customer, to a certain extent, is working in the dark. This creates some unique challenges to the consultative seller:

- Momentum to change is very slow. The customer doesn't know what he doesn't know and is very unlikely to buy until his eyes have been opened.
- More than any other role, the consultative seller requires the greatest skill in communicating. This is because the representative is asked to establish credibility and trust, explore business issues intelligently, and provide solutions in a form palatable to senior management.
- The consultative seller is always at risk. While he may develop the need for a product or service, that doesn't guarantee selection as the supplier. Additionally, consultative sellers must be careful not to come across as too smart or professional. They must walk the fine line that all good consultants walk: the line that facilitates a solution to problems rather than solving them personally.

The essence, then, of the consultative seller role is that it is a problem-driven approach. The consultative role concerns itself with addressing and reducing organizational problems *with* the customer. This differs from the negotiator role, which, as you'll see in the next chapter, is interest driven. By that I mean the sale will relate more to the *individual* interest of the buyer than the needs of the *organization*. Two examples may serve to demonstrate this difference.

Let's suppose you were approached by two sales representatives. The first is trying to sell health maintenance organizations (HMOs) as an alternative to your traditional health insurance. The other is trying to sell you auto insurance.

Now, what do you know about HMOs? If you're like me, probably very little. You've had traditional insurance all your life. Little Tommy had his tonsils removed just last year and the plan covered all but a hundred bucks. Why rock the boat? If you talk to the salesperson at all, it will probably be with a very skeptical attitude.

What about car insurance? Well, that's different.

You've bought plenty of insurance before. You know all about deductibles, liability, and personal injury coverages. And what about that claim you made two years ago? Your present carrier didn't respond quite as quickly as you would have liked. If this guy can give you the same coverage for less—hell, even if he's just a nice guy—you'll probably give him the business.

Clearly, the approaches of the two sales reps must be different. To generate interest in an HMO, the sales rep would have to *develop* needs by exploring current and potential problems with your coverage. This might relate to medical expenses not covered by your present policy because of a deductible, preventative checkups that are not fully reimbursed, maximum coverages in the case of serious illness, dental and pharmaceutical coverages, or time lags between your payment to a doctor or hospital and reimbursement from the insurance company. These are all issues that are not actively on your mind at any given time. The good consultative seller acts as a catalyst to start you thinking, then develops that line of thought into a need for a change. In the case of the auto insurance, you and the sales rep are more or less on even ground. The rep must present the advantages of his approach over a competitor but he doesn't have to explore every facet of your coverage.

When is the consultative role appropriate? The consultative role is a difficult role for most salespeople to master. It's time consuming, a bit risky, and not always necessary. It's an appropriate role to assume when:

- The product or service is truly new to customers. Examples might include truly new technology, new services (like the HMO), or some new combination of features.
- When the market is new. Examples might include data processing to small businesses, employee stock plans to large companies, or management services to government.
- When a marketing decision has been made to approach the market with a "concept." An example of this is American Express's attempts to link its travel agency services with its corporate credit card to create a "Travel Management System." This is appropriate only

if the marketing department has truly "packaged" the concept into a demonstrable product.

Selling in the Consultative Role

To sell in this role you must be able to:

- Recognize problems within the customer's organization.
- *Develop* needs with the customer—not simply uncover them.
- Provide solutions to the problem, not simply benefits of the product.
- Communicate solutions in a format that the customer understands.

As a consultative seller, it's essential that you be able to recognize symptoms and project probable causes in the operations that relate to your product or service. If, for example, you sell data processing services that can reduce the personnel time required to issue a check through accounts payable, you should be able to recognize that piles of ledgers, manual entries, errors, and a frazzled bookkeeper are symptoms of an inefficient, uncontrolled system.

How do you accomplish this? As in most sales situations the first step is to know your product. But you must know it in three dimensions:

1. Features, functions, and applications. If you sell copiers, know the essentials such as how many copies per minute it makes, what copying process it uses, and special applications like color copying and odd-shaped documents.
2. Benefits to users, managers, and perhaps customers. This often takes the form of a "since . . . you'll be able . . ." approach. For example, "Since our copier produces 100 copies per minute, you'll be able to duplicate field bulletins faster."
3. Value-added benefits. These are the advances the company or department can realize from the purchase. These advances generally revolve around fundamental issues like productivity, cost efficiencies, reduced stress, or quality. The use of firm percentage

savings and actual examples are extremely effective in
making this type of case.

Consultative sellers see the sale as you might see a ship through
the wrong end of a telescope. The product explanation looms way
off in the distance. In the foreground are all the pressing concerns
of the customer. What are these concerns? To a certain extent that
depends on what you sell. To the retailer it may be gross margins,
to the office manager—budget control, to the physician—patient
compliance. To the consultative seller this is the stuff of change.
Remember, we defined consultative sellers as those individuals
who sell you something you didn't know you were going to buy. So
change becomes an essential element in the sale.

The Consulting Needs of Different Buying Levels

So the next step in becoming an effective consultative seller is
defining those areas of the customer's operation that your product
or service can address. As I said, this will depend to some extent on
what you sell, but it is possible to make some broad assumptions
about the needs of different buyers:

1. Performance Buyers. These are the people who will
    actually use or supervise the use of the product or
    services. The fundamental business concerns of these
    people will actually be very personal since their
    reputation may be intimately connected to the per-
    formance of the product or service. Hence, they will
    be interested in reliability, ease of use, training, ser-
    vice availability, and breakdown time.
2. Middle Managers. As I said earlier, middle managers
    differ from their senior counterparts in a fundamental
    way: since they are on the line, they must often make
    decisions quickly and without benefit of clear delinea-
    tion of the causes of a problem or alternate solutions.
    Hence, their decisionmaking process has elements of
    the performance buyer and the senior manager. Their
    interests are likely to include improved efficiencies,
    reduced costs, improved morale, reduced stress, and
    reduced errors.

You may have noticed the heavy reliance on the words *improved* and *reduced*. This is a fundamental to understanding the needs of middle managers. They live for the short term (at least at work). They are responsible for producing *now*. Their minds are focused on how the operation is running now. They stay up nights wondering how the operation can be improved or how problems can be reduced or eliminated. Theirs is a universe of costs, efficiencies, and processes.

3. Senior Managers. These people live in a universe that's different from yours or mine. Their responsibilities are global and their means of measuring success may seem a bit arcane to you. They differ from the middle manager in seemingly minor but actually important ways. These people listen when you discuss productivity (versus efficiency), return on investment (versus reduced costs), customer satisfaction (versus improved morale), and production capacity (versus reduced errors).

Keep in mind that while selling consultatively, it's vital to line yourself up with your buyer. The senior manager does not actually see production going on; therefore, to speak in specific terms about efficiencies would be fruitless. They do, however, review figures on productivity or units produced per work hour. They're not vitally concerned with *how* productivity is achieved (presumable through efficiencies) but simply that one worker produces more than previously. The same is true with money. Most senior managers don't have a line item budget that must be adhered to at all costs. They do, however, have responsibility for ensuring that all the company's assets are used wisely.

So it's a matter of perspective with senior versus middle managers. For the former it's "big picture" and somewhat conceptual; for the latter it's immediate and instantly demonstrable.

Opening the Consultative Sales Call

Obviously, much of what goes into opening a call in the consultative role depends on where you are in the sales cycle. If you are meeting a customer for the first time, for example, you'll open the sale differently than you would if you had called on her 20 times previously. However, no matter what stage of the sales cycle you are in, there are two critical objectives that must be realized in every opening:

1. Trust
2. Credibility

Keep in mind that you are trying to position yourself as someone who can help a customer with her business. Think about that for a moment. Who are you to tell anybody about *their* business? You're just a sales representative, remember? Many customers, unfortunately, are going to look at you in just those terms. So those first 60 seconds are going to be critical to the success of the consultative approach. Let's look, then, at these two critical objectives—trust and credibility.

Trust

Trust is an elusive quality, particularly in today's selling environment. Let's face it. Not all salespeople enjoy the best reputations. Like it or not, some people will automatically lump you together with some of these less scrupulous people. To many people, when you say the words "sales representative" images of broken promises, overstated claims, and overaggressive behavior are immediately conjured up. You and I both know that this image is largely unfair, that most salespeople care deeply about their accounts and really want to serve them well. However, since the image exists you have to do things to overcome it.

Think about the people you trust. What qualities do they exhibit that make them trustworthy? Probably foremost on your list would be a track record of delivering on promises—no matter what the circumstances. Second on many people's lists would be a true concern for the well-being of others. Third might be an honest straightforward approach to dealing with people, the ability to tell people when they're right and point out their faults as well.

Unfortunately, you do not have the luxury of a track record with most of your customers, particularly the new ones. In fact, you may be fighting a negative track record established by a predecessor or earlier company policies. As a result, you'll have to establish trust by exhibiting a real concern for the customer's well-being and being straightforward and honest. Here are some techniques that consultative sellers use when opening a call with a *new* customer:

- Focus your opening on *general* business needs. For example; "Mr. Smith, many department heads find that centralized copier services result in a serious loss of productivity as secretaries and even professionals spend a great deal of time on line waiting for the copier to come free. Have you found this to be a problem in your department?" An opening like this allows you to focus the customer's attention on a problem rather than on you. The statement is a standard problem that many customers face. It will require an answer from the customer and will get a dialogue started.

- Try to use the case history approach to starting the dialogue. This might be an actual or fictitious scenario of how a similar operation benefited from dealing with you. For example: "Last year I was dealing with a marketing department very much like yours. It found it had a tremendous lag time between the time personnel submitted artwork to the art department and the time they received camera-ready text. What's the typical lag time in your department?" This sort of approach establishes that you have worked with marketing departments before and that you have some understanding of their operation. As in the previous example, you are involving the customer almost immediately.

- Take the straightforward approach. Admit to ignorance, if appropriate. For example: "Ms. Jones, I'm confident that we can help you with your copier needs but I'll need to find out a few things about your operation. Would you mind if I asked you a few questions?"

- The third-party referral technique also works well. For example: "We recently installed a copier for Mr.

Thomas in accounting and significantly increased productivity. He mentioned that you had expressed some dissatisfaction with your current copier setup—is that true?" Two points to remember when using a third-party referral: (1) mention what you did to help the party to whom you're referring and (2) make sure the party is known and respected by the current customer.

- Establish a limited objective that will demonstrate your trustworthiness. For example: "Ms. Brown, I'd like to talk to you about setting the parameters for a study of your copying activity. Then I'd like to put those parameters in writing for your review next Thursday." This sort of opening allows you to complete a simple sales task and demonstrate that you deliver on your promises without "pushing" the customer too far.

These techniques only get you started on the road to establishing trust. Clearly, the only true way to establish trust is over the long term, by following up on promises and by delivering what you say you'll deliver. To establish trust on calls other than the initial call, follow these techniques:

- Summarize the results of your last call. For example: "Mr. Ford, on my last call, you stated the need for improved color resolution on copiers and asked that I supply you with samples of how our model 9800 could help you in this area. You also said that you wanted verification of our improved service record. Can we take a few moments to review these two requests?"
- After you've reviewed the follow-up items, bridge to your next objective by using one of the techniques discussed earlier.

Trust *is* an elusive commodity but by relentlessly following up on your promises and by using these techniques, you will begin to establish it with your customer base.

Credibility

If trust is elusive, credibility is an absolute mystery. Politicians and world leaders grapple with the problem of being credible all

the time and frankly, most never really master it. There are a
number of elements to remember when trying to establish
credibility: (1) You don't have to know *everything*. You ARE expected to know your products and their appropriate applications.
You are NOT expected to understand every facet of a customer's
operation. (2) Credibility is not established by stating *credentials*. I
once traveled with a bank calling officer (the person in a bank who
calls on corporate treasurers to sell them financing and other
finanical management services). This young man was extremely
bright, energetic, and well educated. He felt that he could impress
a corporate treasurer with his background and thus open the door
to some meaningful dialogue. He proceeded to open the call with a
list of his educational accomplishments as well as the full extent of
his training at the bank. The treasurer, a gray-haired, dis-
tinguished gentleman, listened patiently and then said: "You know
I never got the opportunity to finish college. It was the depression
and I had to go out and find a job. I started here as a junior
bookkeeper before we had all these computers and things. I really
feel the best way to learn anything is by *doing* it. Have you been
doing this long?" The young man, obviously flustered, had to admit
that he had only been at it for three months and had not yet been
able to structure a real financial package. (3) Credibility is established by *delivering* not by talking about it. However, here are
some techniques that can get you on the road to establishing
credibility:

- Try to solve a simple problem first. If you have seen
  other departments or companies employ a procedure
  that works well, share it with the customer at the
  earliest possible opportunity.
- Use the case history approach to demonstrate your
  understanding of problems and concerns.
- Use your organization. Even if you have an answer
  immediately, withhold it and say: "I think *we* might be
  able to help you with that. Let me talk to our customer
  service department." This approach will ensure that
  you don't come across as a "know it all" and will also
  demonstrate that your organization supports its salespeople.
- Support statements you make with quotes or refer-

ences from trade journals or other literature. For example: "The American Marketing Association recently stated that the need for first class graphic reproduction was a primary concern of its membership." Sad to say, but the fact that you actually read will probably set you in better stead with your customers than many of your competitors.

• Ask questions. Truly credible people let others do the talking more than talking themselves. Ask customers how things work and *listen* to their explanations, making remarks only from time to time. An inquiring mind will never hurt you when you're trying to establish your credibility.

Opening the consultative sales call is a critical skill that many people find extremely difficult to master. It involves showing concern for the customer while not seeming too anxious to sell something. This channeling of energy *toward* the customer's operation and away from selling the product proves too much for many salespeople. One successful salesperson I was working with stated that she simply put the product out of her mind for the first three calls she made on the customer. She treated those calls as a learning experience where she could come to know the intricacies of various operations. Once fueled with that knowledge, she felt that she could really get into the detail of application that her product required. Now your selling environment may not allow for that pace of selling; however, a strong customer-oriented approach to the sale will inevitably lead to a more consultative role in your selling.

A Consultative Probing Strategy

Once the climate for consultation has been established, you must actually be able to start the consultative process. In every situation I have been involved in, that process begins with an examination of needs. The method for examining needs is probing—or asking questions. Many feel that probing is the *only* selling skill a salesperson really needs. That may be true, but its been my experience that *what* is being probed is the fundamental issue—not the simple fact that probing is taking place.

In order to begin effective probing as a consultative seller it's necessary to take another look at the concept of *need*. Within the selling environment, we can define need as any expression of wants, concerns, or desires that a customer may express about his operation. Generally, these will be statements of change aimed at improving the operation. These improvements would be based on the buyer's analysis of the situation and knowledge of possible solutions. Keeping in mind what we know about the consultative role—namely, that you are selling something the customer didn't know he was going to buy—how reliable is the customer's analysis and knowledge of solutions?

Let's suppose you're selling computers to small businesses who have never had a computer before. You're aware of the time savings that an inventory control system can accomplish. But to the buyers it's all "new fangled technology." If you simply asked the buyers what they need, they'd never come up with an automated approach. They simply don't have the knowledge necessary to make that decision. In order to use the consultative approach, you must look at need as a two-tiered entity.

> Tier 1—Everyday Needs. These are the needs that plague every business person. Their operations are never efficient enough, their people are never competent enough, there's never enough money, or staff, or time in the day to get everything accomplished.
>
> Tier 2—Urgent Needs. These are the needs that must be addressed immediately or the entire operation will be at jeopardy.

Clearly, greater opportunity exists when needs are at least perceived as urgent by the customers. This is why it's often such a pleasure to deal with intelligent customers. They're often able to see the urgency of problems sooner. Unfortunately, you can't choose who your customers will be.

The art of consultative selling involves moving the customer from the everyday to the urgent and then providing solutions. This is accomplished through a probing strategy that moves through various levels, leading the customer to a full analysis of the operation. There are essentially four levels to this probing strategy:

Level 1—Fact Finding

Level 2—Feel Finding

Level 3—Impact Investigation

Level 4—Solution Inquiry

Keep in mind that this strategy is meant to create a sense of urgency in the buyer's mind. This sense of urgency will increase the likelihood that action will be taken or—put another way—a sale will be made.

Let's examine each level more closely.

Fact finding is the simple act of determining what's going on in the account. These questions relate to the situation within the account and provide fuel for more in-depth probing later. Some examples of fact-finding probes are: "How many employees work in the department?" "What kind of equipment do you currently use?" "What are you paying for supplies?" "How much overtime do you incur on a weekly basis?" These questions are flat. By that I mean they require no analysis on the part of the customer. The customer at this point is simply acting as a conduit of information that could be retrieved from other sources. An important consideration in the use of fact-finding questions is not to ask too many of them. If you do, the customer may feel that you're taking advantage of her and probably move to terminate the dialogue.

Feel finding increases the involvement of the customer by asking for some preliminary analysis of the situation. These are simple analytical questions, designed to break the surface and set the stage for more thorough analysis later. Some examples might be: "Are you satisfied with your current levels of productivity?" "Do you feel that the department enjoys a positive image with the rest of the organization?" "Are you happy with the current process?" This analysis involves getting the customer's attitudes and feelings on a given situation. The result of this line of questioning should be the establishment of some pretty strong everyday needs. A major difference between consultative sellers and other salespeople is that consultative sellers don't stop here: they recognize that because a buyer is dissatisfied with something doesn't mean he is ready to act on it. They pursue it further by beginning an impact investigation.

Impact investigation attempts to lead the customer through an in-depth analysis of the *impact* of her *current* dissatisfactions on the *future* of the organization. This is accomplished by establishing a core of business concerns that your product or service can address, then asking how the current problem will impact those concerns. I'll be discussing that core of concerns in more detail in a moment. When the full impact of a problem is aired the consultative seller then makes a solution inquiry.

Solution inquiry involves summarizing the stated needs and then asking if the customer would be interested in some solutions. For example: "Mr. Smith, we've agreed that you want to improve the overall efficiency of your department in order to reduce stress, costs, and improve overall turnaround time for client projects. If I could show you a way to improve efficiency by 25%, would you be interested?" The solution inquiry question is a lot like the traditional close that you may have been exposed to in training classes or discussions with other salespeople. It's different though in two ways: (1) You don't wait until the end of the call to ask it. You can ask a solution inquiry question whenever you feel you've moved the customer from the level of everyday to urgent need. (2) It doesn't really ask the customer to *act*, as in signing an order or conducting a study. It simply asks him to listen or consider. This is an important distinction because it's a lot easier to listen or consider than it is to act in most environments and making it easy on the customer is something the consultative seller strives for all the time.

What this probing strategy does is allow the customer to make a full review of her operation with only gentle prodding from the sales representative. The *cumulative* effect of this approach, however, is quite dramatic:

1.   The customer has done a pretty complete analysis of her operation including the current state of affairs, her attitudes on the situation, and the consequences of not taking action on current problems.

2.   The customer's attention has been heightened because of this dialogue. She's *looking* for solutions instead of bracing herself for a "sales pitch."

3.   The fact that you have been asking intelligent questions about *her* operation establishes you as a credible resource—someone whose ideas may have merit. This makes your discussions of solutions and benefits a lot more tolerable.

4.   Finally, the customer has really set herself up for the close. She's opened up to you about all kinds of things and stated her feelings quite frankly. As long as what you have to offer satisfies her needs, there's really very little room for her to maneuver.

This is an approach first developed by Socrates in ancient Greece to facilitate logical thought with his students.

While this is a book on business-to-business selling, an example from our personal lives might be helpful in illustrating how this approach works. Let's suppose, like 50 or 60 million of us, you've developed a small weight problem. Over the years you've put on about 20 pounds that you've been meaning to lose—but just haven't gotten around to it. Suddenly, you're approached by a salesperson from a health spa. A traditional selling approach might go something like this:

Sales Rep: Hello, Mr. Jones, I represent Think Thin Health Spas and I'd like to discuss club membership with you.

You: OK, what have you got?

Sales Rep: Well, we've got lots of innovative programs. May I ask you a few questions?

You: Sure—shoot.

Sales Rep: May I ask how much you weigh right now?

You:	About 190.
Sales Rep:	Are you happy with that weight?
You:	Not really. I think I could stand to lose a few pounds.
Sales Rep:	Oh, how many is a few?
You:	I don't know . . . 10, maybe 20.
Sales Rep:	Well, we have a program that combines sound nutritional advice with a three times a week exercise program that's guaranteed to take 20 pounds off in three months or your money back. How does that sound?
You:	Three times a week? Sounds kind of strenuous. Let me think about it.

By jumping the gun and telling you what he had to offer, the sales rep scared you off. You haven't had time to think about how much you really want to lose the weight. After all, you've been carrying it for years now and it hasn't seemed to have had a really negative effect. In fact, as in most sales encounters, *you're looking for ways to say no rather than yes*. The need is not urgent. Chances are you'll take his literature and file it deeply into some obscure place to "think about later."

Let's see the same scenario taking a more consultative approach.

Sales Rep:	Mr. Jones, I represent Think Thin Health Spas and I'd like to talk to you about establishing a program for fitness and weight control. Would you mind if I asked you a few questions?
You:	No, go ahead.
Sales Rep:	Thanks. Can we start with your present height and weight?
You:	Sure, 5 foot 2; 190 pounds.
Sales Rep:	And your present state of health?
You:	Oh, pretty good I think—though I do seem to be a bit more tired than I'd like.

Sales Rep:	Are you satisfied that this is your ideal weight?
You:	Well, no—not really. I mean I think I could stand to lose a few pounds.
Sales Rep:	May I ask how many?
You:	Well, ideally I'd like to shed about 40 pounds. But I don't want to work too hard at it.
Sales Rep:	Have you considered what the health implications of these 40 pounds might be?
You:	Health?
Sales Rep:	Well, studies have shown a connection between extra weight and heart disease, diabetes, and hypertension.
You:	Oh, yeah, sure.
Sales Rep:	How about the career implications?
You:	Well, I really don't think anybody around here is going to hold a few extra pounds against me.
Sales Rep:	Perhaps not, but many organizations have a sort of unspoken bias against people with a few extra pounds.
You:	Well, actually the VP has been giving me a lot of grief at meetings lately.
Sales Rep:	Are the social aspects of this problem a concern to you?
You:	Social?
Sales Rep:	Well, we are in a health conscious society. People carrying a few extra pounds are often stigmatized. How about the economic aspects of this problem?
You:	Economic?
Sales Rep:	You know, things like tailoring clothes, changing styles to improve the fit—things like that.

You: Woll, I *havo* had to. . . .

Sales Rep: If I could show you a low-cost, no-risk way to lose those pounds and improve your overall health—would you be interested?

You: Tell me more.

By leading you through an examination of your small weight problem, the sales rep was able to have you examine the health, career, social, and economic impacts of your situation. What was once something you wanted to do something about *some* day has now been expanded to a major danger to health and happiness. Which approach do you think has a greater probability of success?

Developing a Core of Business Concerns

Just as the health spa salesperson developed a core of concerns relating to the health, social, career, and economic impacts of a weight problem, so must you develop a similar core for your product or service. This core becomes the environment for the complete exploration of the customer's problems and dissatisfactions. By having this core developed ahead of time, you can easily spring into an impact inquiry without seeming to strain for questions. This is important in light of the consultative seller's concern for trust and credibility. If you can easily lead a dialogue that is of major concern to a customer, how can you miss increasing your credibility?

These core concerns are determined to a large extent by two factors:

1. The level of management on which you're calling.
2. The type of businesses on which you're calling.

Sales Call and the Level of Management

I discussed the differences between different levels of management earlier in this chapter. You'll recall that I said that performance buyers usually have a very immediate perspective on the product or service. They don't want to look bad and therefore take a very personal approach to the sale. Middle managers, on the other hand, must make decisions for a broader clientele and yet are often unable to conduct careful analysis for the solution to problems. They want fast, easy-to-understand solutions and good follow-up. Finally, senior managers are responsible for the company's assets and must take a more global view of any purchase decision. Hence, they look at overall return on investment, productivity enhancements, and reductions of overall organizational costs.

Sales Call and the Type of Business

The type of industry you call on is equally important to the development of this core of concerns. In order to develop the right core for you, it's important to know how your customers measure the success and failure of their operations.

There are many ways to measure the effectiveness of a business operation. Many are obscure and beyond the range of this book. However, you probably won't go wrong if you develop your core of concerns in three primary areas:

1. Financial
2. Productivity
3. Satisfaction

Different industries and different buyer types will measure these factors differently. Let's examine some of these measurements for three industry types—retail, commercial or office, and industrial.

Retail

The retail environment of today is perhaps the most competitive of any business. Margins are often razor thin and a single purchasing mistake can make the difference between an entire operation succeeding or failing. The failures of such giants as W. T. Grants and the problems experienced by such household names as A & P and Woolworths are ample evidence that today's retailer must be cautious and smart. As a result, these businesses have established procedures and controls that are second to none in assuring the success of purchase decisions. Sophisticated retailers can now determine what's selling and what's not on an almost minute-by-minute basis through the use of checkout computers and inventory control systems. This has resulted in extremely informed buying decisions at every level of the organization.

On the performance buyer level, the retail buyer is concerned with raw sales as the means of measuring financial success or failure. These are the store-level people given the responsibility for an aisle or department of the store. If an item is not moving, it will not last long. In the area of productivity, these individuals will be concerned with shelf and display management. Concerns revolve around who will maintain the shelf when it comes to restocking or cleaning packages, who will maintain point of sale, and other merchandising questions. Finally, they measure satisfaction primarily by consumer remarks.

Retail *middle managers*, such as store managers and headquarters' buyers, take a slightly more sophisticated approach. They measure the success or failure of a product by the number of times a product turns in a week, month, or year. They are very concerned with the margins to be realized on the product and how often they have to promote the price in order to move the goods. They look at a product in terms of the amount of sales it produces in relation to the amount of space it takes up in the store. They measure productivity in terms of the amount of couponing that goes on for a given product. This is a time-consuming exercise that is well worth it *if* the product moves as a result. They also look closely at the merchandising time involved in terms of building displays and maintaining point of sale material. They measure satisfaction primarily through consumer remarks and sales figures.

Finally, *senior* managers tend to look at product performance in terms of a number of sophisticated financial management techniques such as Gross Margin Return on Investment (GMROI). They are also concerned with their overall market share, profit contribution, and the results of such research companies as Nielsen and SAMI.

Commercial or Office

The office environment of today is in a total state of flux. Technological innovations such as the personal computer and advanced communications systems are changing white collar work in ways never before imagined. Still, the office environment maintains many of the same management procedures that have served it so well for so long.

Office equipment or service performance buyers such as secretaries and office managers usually do not have any strong financial concerns. They may have operating budgets to adhere to, but the major responsibility for that will come from middle managers. They are very concerned, however, with productivity issues. These often include how many tasks an office worker can perform in an hour as well as the number of *steps* required to complete a task. If working with equipment, they are very concerned with downtime as well as the quality of service support available. In the area of satisfaction, they are most concerned with the remarks of their "client" base, whether they be executives using secretarial services or field operations utilizing data processing support functions. Reduced stress and ease of use are also high on the user's list of satisfaction measurements.

Middle managers in the office environment are generally very price or discount conscious, since they must adhere to operating budgets and guidelines. Their productivity measurements generally deal with the amount of work a clerical worker can produce in a given time frame as well as the amount of time professionals must spend in clerical tasks. They measure satisfaction from the responses of their client groups and by looking at stress levels, absentee reports, and turnover statistics.

When *senior managers* look at the office, they tend to think in terms of return on investment, depreciation, and amortization of equipment. If they are looking at a service, they are concerned with lowering price by utilizing volume. In the productivity arena, they look toward reducing headcount for a given job function as well as analyzing the production per work hour for various job titles. They are also vitally concerned with the activity of their professionals because this represents a major investment in any company.

Industrial

The industrial sector differs from the office sector only in the fact that it is more advanced in its management techniques. Despite the bad press that American management endures, the factory is probably second only to the retail operation in terms of its comfort with technology and improving productivity.

Performance buyers in the industrial sector usually have little or no financial concerns except as they might relate to wastage or some operating budget line items. They are intimately concerned, however, with such productivity items as equipment downtime, service, and units produced per work hour. They measure satisfaction through ease of use of equipment or services and, to an increasing degree, quality.

In the industrial sector, *middle managers* are becoming increasingly sophisticated in their ability to measure effectiveness. In the financial area, they are concerned with price per unit bought as well as available discounts for volume. They are increasingly concerned with inventory levels and the cost of that inventory in terms of "just in time" management principles. Their productivity measures center largely on units produced per work hour and equipment downtime. They measure satisfaction by listening to employee comments, as well as analyzing the quality of the products produced.

Finally, *senior managers* tend to measure success and failure in terms of return on investment, depreciation, and amortization as well as an overall impact on production costs. They review units produced per work hour and grapple with headcount considerations when reviewing productivity. Their satisfaction measurement must take into account labor relations and quality issues.

Presenting a Business Case

Clearly, to be a consultative seller you must have considerably more at your disposal than the simple skill of asking questions. It's true that you must be adept at communicating, but you must also be very aware of the operations of your customers. Equally important, you must be able to decide when to pursue an avenue of opportunity and when to let it go. Because you are *facilitating* the customer's thought patterns, you must learn patience and discretion.

The final consideration in the consultative selling role is presenting information about your product or service. The traditional route of presenting features and benefits is appropriate here with some modification. Traditionally, we have been trained to think of products in terms of what it can do for the customer. An example might be "because of our easy-load feature, you can realize substantial time savings." That sort of statement can be received positively or it can lead to objections. What sets the consultative seller apart is the *timing* of the product presentation. In many sales, as soon as there is an opening, the salesperson will begin a discussion of the product. The feeling is that the sooner such a discussion can take place, the sooner the customer will make a decision. In the consultative sale, the seller waits until she is certain that the needs have been made urgent in the buyer's mind. This is accomplished through the solution inquiry in the probing strategy. If the customer answers "yes"—he would like to see some ideas on solving the problem—then you're ready to begin a discussion of the product.

Is a simple description of features and benefits enough? Not totally. Let's keep in mind that when selling in the consultative role, your customer is still feeling his way. You *have* moved him into a realm that will probably be conducive to purchase. Yet at base, the customer does not fully understand your product. So instead of jumping into a description of what your product can do, it's smart to take the business case approach to the presentation. The business approach involves three steps:

1. Summary of needs
2. Recommended solutions
3. Documentation

The **summary of needs** should be made using language as close to the customer's own as possible. If there are terms for procedures or tasks, use them as part of the summary. This will allow you to not only make sure you have all the facts but also to demonstrate your listening abilities and credibility.

Your **recommended solutions** should be pegged only to the needs stated. Even if your product has more capabilities—stay away from them. They will come as a pleasant surprise if the buyer buys, and fuel for handling objections if he doesn't.

Documentation should include any proof sources you have developed earlier as well as satisfied customer testimonials. If claims are not disputed—don't try to prove them.

If this presentation can be made in writing, all the better. But no matter what the circumstances, follow these steps in order to receive the maximum attention.

Closing the Consultative Sales Call

Since the consultative seller sells solutions rather than products, the close of a consultative call is different from a more traditional selling approach. Traditionally, a sales call ends with a call to action. The action might be to sign an order, view a demonstration, or accept a sample.

The consultative close also ends with a call to action. But it's a call to solve problems, investigate solutions, or address dissatisfactions. This is a critical difference. Unlike a traditional close, which may be asking the customer to act in a way he hadn't yet considered (like signing an order), the consultative close is a logical extension of the conversation that has just taken place. So instead of closing on the product, close on the solution. For example, instead of saying, "Would you agree to a demonstration of our copier to show how clear the copying image is?" try "Since we've agreed that your current copying image is a problem, would you agree to a demonstration to see how our system can address this problem?" With this approach, the customer is agreeing to solve *his* problem not accepting *your* capabilities. And that's a lot easier to do. Again, if you've got the product and it really can solve his problem, signing the order will almost take care of itself.

Summary

The consultative role in selling is not an easy one to master. If you find yourself in this type of selling environment, give it time. These are skills that the best consultative salespeople have taken years to master. With the proliferation of products and services, however, this approach may be the best hope you have of differentiating yourself and gaining the customers' attention in a crowded marketplace.

5

THE SALES NEGOTIATOR

Needs versus Interests

The vast majority of salespeople conduct business in an environment where major portions of the sales outcome are known before selling takes place. They sell products or services that are so vital to their customers that *not* buying is simply out of the question. These products are quite simply necessary for the company to continue doing business. Retailers *must* carry certain brands or face the wrath of their consumers, automobile companies *must* buy steel, at least until they perfect the plastic car, offices must have paper and supplies, and so on. Both buyers and sellers know this, and it shades the way they do business. The sale in this environment is not *whether* the account will buy but *how much* and from *whom*. Consequently, certain environmental factors have developed. For example:

- Most buying accounts have established guidelines and procedures for the purchase of these goods or services.
- Purchasing authority is generally given to people at lower levels in the organization.
- Buyers are appraised not so much on the quality of what they buy as the terms they're able to extract from suppliers.
- Multiple supplier relationships are considered desirable.

Sales negotiators are engaged in trying to change or expand these procedures and guidelines for the purpose of gaining entry for their products or services. They are asked to develop terms that are both attractive to the buyer and protective of their own interests. In addition, they are expected to find ways to gain competitive advantage over the other suppliers in the account.

Since the outcome is more or less given, there is generally less need to examine needs with the buyer. These purchases have been made so often that there's a good chance the buyer may know as much or more about the product than the seller does. Instead, the sales negotiator tries to deal with short-term *interests* in order to gain a foothold.

Interests are defined as *short-term concerns, problems, or ambitions that the buyer may have—at the time sales decisions are being made.* Interests differ from needs in that they are more individual than organizational. There are a number of reasons why sales negotiators concentrate on interests.

1. Because these goods or services are purchased so regularly, the organization as a whole has, to a certain extent, lost interest in the buying decision. As long as the specifications are met, most people don't care if they use one brand of paper over another.
2. Since the buying decision is often made by lower-level officials, such as purchasing agents or line supervisors, and since this level of the organization works "under fire," they're often unable to give decisions careful analysis; they tend to make decisions that will solve *today's* problem and cover them politically.
3. Because so many competitive suppliers are offering incentives, the buyers' are constantly changing their criteria for vendor selection.

These factors work in harmony to make the face-to-face encounter with the buyer extremely important to the sales negotiator.

The Tools for Determining Interests

In order to examine interests effectively, buyers and sales negotiators must:

- Exchange information
- Leverage power

Exchanging Information

The exchange of information is accomplished in the usual way—
through asking questions. It's important to know the areas of
interest that any buyer may bring to a sales negotiation. Typically,
the buyer will, either formally or informally, establish standards for
most products or services. These standards may include competitive prices, prompt, flexible delivery, responsive service, warranties, and possibly customized billing options and usage reports.
Underlying those interests, however, are some very human interests that the savvy sales negotiator also recognizes: interests like
recognition, security, and organizational acceptance. While the
outward selling concentrates on the former set of interests, the real
decision is often made on the latter. The sales negotiator capitalizes
on this second set of interests through the second activity—
leveraging power.

Leveraging Power

As was said earlier, the buyers appear to be dealt a better hand
in sales negotiations. After all, they have the money, access to
other suppliers, and, perhaps most importantly, the *authority* to
say yes or no. But do they really? Let's examine their power a little
more closely. The money after all is not really theirs; it's the
organizations. Nothing will set a purchasing agent scrambling like a
call from an executive who has determined that a competitor is
getting a better "deal." The buyer can release funds but they really
can't *spend* the company's money in the same way they can spend
their paycheck on whatever they want. What about their authority
to say yes or no? Here again, most buyers are walking on pretty
thin ice. Within the parameters of their jobs they *can* agree to a
sale, sign an order, or grant an interview. But what do you think
senior executives would think of a buyer who refused to see legitimate suppliers on a regular basis? Who trusted one supplier to
communicate all the changes within an industry? Do you think
such a buyer would last long in most of today's organizations? Of
course not. So that leaves only one real power base—the ability to
call in other suppliers. The onus falls on you to minimize that
power.

What about your power base? Are you—the lowly peddler—
capable of bringing any power to a sales negotiation? You bet you

are! And it's not illusory power like the buyers. First and foremost of your powers is the power of information. Some negotiating experts maintain that information is the *only* power you need. It's certainly a formidable thing to have—and you have it in abundance. Every time you make a sales call you're adding to that power base by listening to customers, coming to understand their operations, and keeping an eye on what the competition is up to. In most cases, your customer is chained to the desk and may get out to see what's going on only a few times a year at trade association meetings or shows. Most of them would give their right arm to know as much as you do about the marketplace. You have other bases of power as well. An important one is the product or service you're selling. When I was in the car rental business, nothing used to give me more pleasure than a phone call from a customer who would barely speak to me during the year, begging me to find a car for an executive headed for some popular destination at the last minute. These sorts of encounters, no matter how rare, graphically point out the dependency of buyers on all suppliers within a marketplace. Your ability to influence pricing and delivery decisions within your own company is also a formidable base of power. No buyer, no matter how big, can really influence the price paid for goods or services. The best they can hope to do is play one supplier against another in the hopes that one will lower a price or expedite a delivery schedule. Unfortunately, many suppliers often fail to realize this and give in too easily.

By recognizing these bases of power and utilizing them, you begin to appeal to the more personal interests of a buyer. However, it's important to use them subtly. To take a position, for instance, like "I'll walk out, if I don't get my way" doesn't work in labor negotiations and it certainly won't work in a sales negotiation. Instead, try to insert the fact that you know what's going on in the marketplace into general conversation. Start a meeting by discussing an installation at another account. If a customer wants to know about a certain product, tell her you'll have to check availability. And if, by some chance, a customer should request a meeting, try to put her off for a day or two—no matter how badly you need the business. By making a conscious effort to remind customers continually of your bases of power, you increase the likelihood that they will begin to say to themselves, "Perhaps this is a company I should know more about."

Planning a Sales Negotiation

Sales negotiations require a certain amount of planning before meeting with the customer. You should keep in mind that in most cases a successful sales negotiation will not be accomplished in one call. After all, you're trying to break an organization's old habits and routines. I can't tell you how long the sale should take for you. Only you know your business that well. In most cases, however, it will require multiple calls to make any meaningful headway in a high-level sales negotiation. With such an investment of time and your company's money, it's important to know where you're headed. So I'd strongly recommend developing a strong negotiating plan before approaching major accounts. An effective plan of attack should consider these elements:

1. Introducing the company
2. Determining objectives
3. Determining interests and criteria
4. Developing positions
5. Developing a settlement range

Introducing the Company

The obvious place to start a sales negotiation is with an *introduction of yourself and the company*. When planning your opening, it's important to remember these three techniques:

- Recognize the current suppliers. This sends a message to the buyer that you are ready to negotiate and that you probably know a great deal about his current arrangement. An example might be: "Mr. Smith, I'm Francine Jones from Allied Steel. Allied is very anxious to do business with you and would like to have the opportunity to explore a business relationship. I understand that you are currently using Sagamore Steel and Denton Steel—is that correct?"
- Demonstrate your power of information. It's important to establish your power bases as early in the encounter as possible. If you know the customer's current deal, use that information. For example: "My information is

that you are currently receiving a 10% discount from both Sagamore and Denton—is that correct?" Many buyers will respond to that sort of statement with phrases like "You certainly do your homework." Others may become a bit defensive, but that's all right too, because if the buyer is secretive, it's better to know it up front than find it out later. If you don't know the customer's current deal, use what you do know. For example: "Mr. Smith, we've estimated your volume at about 3000 tons per year; most accounts that size are receiving a discount of 10% from both Sagamore and Denton. Does that approximate your current package?"

- Demonstrate openness and empathy. Since you are going to be dealing with this individual for some time, it's best to demonstrate to him that you will be easy to get along with and open to suggestions. Phrases such as "I'd like your help in determining what constitutes a good package" or "We at Allied feel we can suit a package to any buyer's interests and would welcome the chance to explore alternatives with you" will help create the right atmosphere.
- Seek two-way communication. Get the buyer involved from the beginning. Long monologues on the strengths of your company may be the worst way to open a sales negotiation. Use simple trial questions like "don't you agree" or "does that sound appropriate for your operation?" to increase involvement.

Determining Objectives

Perhaps the most difficult concept for any sales negotiator to master is that one really can't be sure, going in, what the outcome of a sales negotiation will be. A negotiation should be a fluid process where interests are explored and expanded, not a process where firm positions are taken and then staunchly defended. For this reason, your initial call objectives should be almost vague. You should certainly ensure that the negotiating process continues, but beyond that it becomes dangerous to be too specific in stating desired outcomes.

Firm objectives should only be established *with* the customer. When planning this step, follow these guidelines:

- List what you feel should be included in any "arrangement": for example, a flexible pricing package, customized billing and usage reports, and an efficient delivery schedule.
- Plan ways to seek customer reactions. By doing this you reinforce that this will be a *joint* venture between you and the buyer. Plan questions like: "Do you agree that those are the minimum requirements for any arrangement we might develop?"
- Plan to seek *additional* objectives. By doing this you immediately put the customer in the position of providing a definition of a "good deal." You can accomplish this by using phrases like: "Given that those are the basics of a good arrangement, what else do you seek from a supplier?"
- Recognize that you will have to be patient but persistent. The customer may not have ever had to articulate standards or specifications before. Be sure to show a strong interest and write down these additional comments. They will provide the basis for a lot of negotiating power later on. And, by all means, if the customer is being vague or cannot articulate well, seek further definition by using such phrases as: "Could you expand on that?" or "I'm not sure I fully understand what you're saying."
- Finally, plan a summary of the discussion by restating all the objectives.

Determining Interests and Criteria

Objectives state customer requirements in very general terms. In order to get into the real meat of a negotiation, you must begin to understand how this customer feels about the current arrangement and how an effective arrangement is measured in this organization. This is accomplished through an exploration of interests and criteria.

Essentially, what you are trying to do in this step is have the buyer further define the requirements for particular elements of a package you want to sell. For example, if you were going to concentrate on pricing, delivery, billing systems, and usage reports, you'd want to get a firm definition of the buyer's stand on these issues. This can be accomplished by developing ways to probe further. However, you have already solicited a great deal of information from the buyer and there is a possibility that patience may be lost. A statement like "Would you mind if I found out a few more details so that I can put together the best offer possible?" will probably open the door to further discussion.

Criteria are standards against which the performance of a product or service are measured. In the best of all worlds, standards would be set for every product. All the sales representatives would have to do is point out how their products meet or exceed those standards. Unfortunately, buyers are not always so logical. Many are overburdened and haven't given much thought to setting standards. Others simply aren't bright enough and still others have established the wrong standards for getting the job done. However, having a customer's criteria established before beginning a sales negotiation is critical to success. Once the buyer is "on the line" with a statement of criteria, she will be very hard pressed to refuse you once you demonstrate that you can meet or exceed them. So, as often as possible, try to get a customer to give you objective criteria. Here are some techniques for getting that information:

- Accepted industry standards. If your industry has established standards, use them in this portion of the sales negotiation. For example: "The American Society of Travelling Executives has established a maximum two-week time frame for responding to disputed fare claims. Is that acceptable to you?"
- The assumptive approach. This technique tries to leverage your knowledge of the marketplace by bringing up the way *others* do things. For example: "Mr. Smith, other buyers find that once a month central billing for all divisions is the most reliable. Would that work well for your operation?"
- The open approach. This is a straight out question to determine how the buyer currently does things. For example: "Mr. Jones, how do you currently evaluate quality in your steel products?"

- The "current and ideal" technique of questioning. This technique asks a buyer (who may not have given a great deal of thought to how a given supplier performs) to establish standards. It goes something like this: "Mr. Smith, if you could have the perfect billing system, what would it include?" After the customer fantasizes a little you ask: "And how does your current system measure up to this?" The customer is put in the position of defining the current supplier's shortcomings.

Developing a Position

Most successful sales negotiators find that this is a good time to withdraw from the customer and take some time to develop a position. As I said earlier, sales negotiating is *not* a process of establishing positions and then defending them. So then why this section on establishing a position? Clearly, any negotiation must have a starting point, a definition of where you can and cannot go with the customer, based on volume, credit, production, or other constraints. Additionally, some procedure is needed for processing the information gathered during the first three planning stages. Consequently, we can define a position as statements of features that will address customer interests and provide a basis for negotiations.

There are two steps in the development of a position for a negotiation:

1. Matching features to interests
2. Assessing the human side of the negotiation

The first step is fairly simple. Any salesperson should be able to match her product or service to the interests and criteria that the customer has established. If, however, the product cannot fully measure up to the criteria or standards, you must find "exclusives" that may minimize the shortcomings. Exclusives relate to the features within the product that may (1) reduce risk, (2) improve operations, or (3) reduce costs. So in order to fully match features to interests, the sales negotiator must clearly *demonstrate* how the product or service will serve the customer's interests with appropriate proof sources or demonstrations. Alternate benefits must also be developed in case a pure match cannot be realized. Once the interests have been identified and addressed, the sales negotiator must move to the human side of the equation. It would be a mistake to think that all sales negotiations are decided solely on the facts. If that were the case, the best product or service would sell every time. Anyone who has developed a superb proposal, only to see it lost because a better-known competitor is able to prey on a customer's fears, knows that the human side of a negotiation is very important indeed. You can begin to assess the human side of a negotiation by looking at decisionmaking motivation of a buyer. Essentially, most buyers will fall into one of the following categories of decisionmaking motivation:

- "The right way." These buyers are secure in their decisionmaking abilities and authority and try to do what's best for the organization. They probably make a determination based solely on the facts.
- Recognition. These buyers want to make dramatic purchases in order to increase visibility with superiors. Their interests probably center on a spectacular price, improved technology, or other highly visible elements of an arrangement.
- Security. These buyers are reluctant to "rock the boat." Change is painful to them so they'll probably take a great deal of convincing before they stick their necks out.

When developing your position, there are certain strategies you can employ to pave the way for meaningful negotiation.

With *right way* buyers, center the presentation on straight business issues such as return on investment, production efficiencies, or cost reduction. These individuals pride themselves on their professionalism. Capitalize on this by using phrases like "I'm sure I don't have to tell you this, but . . ." or "As I'm sure you've seen in the past. . . ." These kinds of statements reinforce their self-image and make your negotiation run smoothly.

For the *recognition* buyers, it's important that they arm themselves with some facts and figures, particularly as they relate to successes others have enjoyed as a result of doing business with your company. Case history or referral statements such as "Com-

pany X was able to realize a 15% productivity improvement by
going with our service" or "Jack Morris at ABC Company was able
to track a 12% cost reduction over the life of the contract" are
effective with these buyers.

For the *security* minded buyer, it's important to show how a
change of suppliers will not cause significant dislocation while at
the same time stressing the improvement that will occur. Again the
case history is helpful. For example: "We were able to make the
changeover to our system in less than two days at Company Y."
Any statement that helps reduce risk in this buyer's mind is bene-
ficial.

In order to establish a position, you must first be able to forecast
the customer's goals. This is called the *customer goal position* and
can be determined by the customer's comments during the objective and criteria phase of the negotiation. By stating his interests
and specific criteria, a customer has (sometimes unknowingly)
established a position.

It's important to keep in mind that the elements of any position
do not relate to specific features of your product. Because a customer says she wants a 20% discount does not constitute a position.
It's your job to expand that narrow view into the larger view. So, as
we said earlier, price becomes a cost position, delivery becomes an
inventory position, service becomes a downtime/response position, warranties and guarantees become a support position, and
terms and conditions become an accounts payable position. By
expanding positions you avoid the antagonistic haggling that takes
place over specific features. We've all gotten into situations where
we develop an obsession with a specific element of a deal (usually
price) to the point where we've actually walked away from an
otherwise profitable encounter. When that happens, we can say
unequivocally that the negotiation has failed. As long as you're
talking and making progress, no matter how minimal, the negotiation is a success. By concentrating on features, you limit your
ability to talk.

When you have forecasted the customer's goal position, you can
develop your *established supportable position*. This position is
established with a firm eye toward the customer's interests and
your own policies. Clearly, your position must show some advantage over the current supplier. These advantages need not be
dramatic to make progress. If you can show even a thin advantage

In a major interest area, it may be enough to get a foot in the door and that's often all you need. This position is called an established supportable position because it is based on your ability to *support* any position you take. You read earlier of support or proof sources. If you are taking a cost position, be sure you can back it up with examples of other organizations that have realized savings or from industry reports that support you. This backup information is more important than the position itself. The position may change; the supporting documentation cannot. Customers can dispute any position you take, but if they dispute your proof, they're forced to come up with their own. And I guarantee you, eight times out of ten, *yours* will be better. Let's look at a few examples of establishing a supportable position.

Let's suppose the customer has requested a four-day delivery schedule in order to maintain a limited inventory for her manufacturing facilities. The best you can offer is a five-day delivery because of a somewhat antiquated order entry system. The key here would be to concentrate on the inventory management issue rather than the delivery issue. Through your determination of objectives and criteria, you should have been able to find out that the reason for wanting to maintain smaller inventories is cost control. A system of last-minute order entry has been determined to be the most efficient way to accomplish that. But are there other ways? Certainly a lower price would enable the buyer to reduce costs; so would better payment terms or less returns. If you have any of these to offer, include them in the position on inventory. Your position might then be stated as "seven-day delivery at a cost of $15 per gross with a defect level of 1% or less and 60-day terms." The supporting documentation might include a complete description of your order handling process, including any extra steps taken to ensure quality, average cost per unit based on the price, and an analysis of the costs of funds based on 60- rather than 30-day payment terms. Once in the negotiation, you will be able to concentrate on these issues rather than the perceived weakness of delivery.

In another situation, let's suppose you were faced with a customer who currently enjoys an 18% discount on goods from one of your competitors. You can match but not exceed this discount because of company policies. You can, however, provide substantial savings through your computerized order entry system and negotiable terms. Your position might be stated as "16% discount with 60-day terms and a minimum order of 10 gross, deliverable by next day courier at no additional cost." Your support statements would include an analysis of the cost of inventory, the cost of money, and perhaps a comparison of delivery costs.

By expanding any position to its widest possible consequences, you slant the negotiation in your favor by providing more areas for negotiation. By coming in slightly higher on key features, you allow yourself the flexibility of changing the position after a full negotiation has been completed. Which leads to the final step in planning a sales negotiation.

Developing a Settlement Range

A **settlement range** is a description of different positions you might take should the negotiation not go according to plan. These various positions should not be thought of as "fall back positions" or compromises. Rather, they are alternate solutions to the customer's interests. They are developed for two reasons: (1) to maintain a dialogue should your original position meet resistance or (2) to provide a means of expanding or reexamining the customer's *stated* interests and criteria. These settlement range positions must be supported in the same way that your first position is. They must relate to customer interests and criteria and they must be in your own best interests. They can include any addition or deletion of features or services.

It's important not to consider these as "reserve" positions. Your first established supportable position should be your *best* position. Playing games with the customer is not what sales negotiation is all about. As you'll see later, a negotiation can go in many different directions. Having a settlement range established before you go in will allow you to respond quickly to any change in the customer's position.

I can't stress enough the importance of planning a sales negotiation. Your buyers have the luxury of shooting from the hip to a certain extent. After all, they already have a supplier who is probably satisfying most of their interests. You don't have that luxury. A carefully planned approach to a sales negotiation will ensure that you enter the negotiation on an even footing with the customer— and probably in a much stronger position.

Conducting a Sales Negotiation

As I said earlier, a sales negotiation will probably extend over a considerable amount of time. To attempt to close an important sales negotiation on one call is probably not well advised. However, there are some fundamentals that should be followed in any face-to-face sales negotiation including the following:

- Creating a conducive climate
- Stating positions
- Seeking interests and alternatives
- Summarizing and closing

Creating a Conducive Climate

In the first few minutes of a sales negotiation, it's important to establish a climate that is conducive to open and profitable negotiations. Keep in mind that many buyers are confronted with salespeople who are less than professional. They may tend to be a little defensive and standoffish. By taking a few simple steps, you can lessen those negative feelings and open up the atmosphere. A conducive climate can be established by:

- Creating an agenda. If possible, it's a good idea to write an agenda and hand it to the customer early in the call. This should be fairly general and outline the areas of interest developed in earlier calls. If it can't be written, then a statement of what you would like to cover will do. The settlement range developed during the planning phase will serve as a more detailed agenda and should *not* be shared with the customer. By creating an agenda, you demonstrate your planning abilities. You also keep the negotiation on track and gain control of the dialogue. After you have reviewed the agenda, ask the customer if there is anything missing.
- Focusing on interests not people. Too often, negotiations that should be positive break down because of personal dislikes. It's often difficult to overcome these dislikes as customers become entrenched or refuse to

discuss issues intelligently. Most often, this change of focus develops from one or more of three possible inhibitors: mindset, feelings, or communications.

Mindset usually comes from concentrating on your positions rather than interests. It develops when you fail to recognize that the customer's thinking on a particular subject is not just *a* problem in realizing your goals—it's *the* problem. Mindset problems can be overcome in a number of ways: (1) Discuss the differences *and* agreements openly. For example: "Joe, I don't think we'll *ever* agree on optimum inventory levels." (2) Agree to a buyer's position, even if you can't do anything about it. For example: "Frankly, Mary, I agree. Ten-day terms are a bit unreasonable but it shouldn't prevent us from doing business." (3) Allow the other side to save face. This can be accomplished by being self-effacing. For example: "I didn't really know this either until I looked it up." Less threatening language also allows the other side to save face, for example, instead of saying "Your price position is too low for *anyone* to make a profit" ask "Is this price position based on competitive offers?"

Feelings are a critical part of any negotiation. As was discussed earlier, customers come to negotiations with a lot of different motivations; to ignore feelings as an element of a negotiation would be unwise. Fear, anxiety, superiority, greed, and mistrust are just a few of the many feelings that may enter into a negotiation at any time. These are pretty dire feelings and it's easy to lose sight of your interests when they surface and start to focus on the person. This can be overcome by following the RAVE technique: (1) Recognize the feelings. There are only two ways to conduct a negotiation. You can either work together or oppose each other. By recognizing that these feelings exist, you can overlook them and get on with business. (2) Acknowledge them. State that many people have similar feelings. For example: "Many first-time buyers can't believe we can save them that much." Agree to feelings when it doesn't damage you. For example: "I can appreciate your annoyance with all these price changes, but it's really the commodities market that dictates things." (3) Vent them. Allow the customer to release her feelings and don't be shy about letting your own out either. (4) Equalize them. Don't react to blow-ups. When a customer receives a message that emotional outbursts won't elicit a similar response, they'll often back off. Use questions and signs of agreement like nodding to show you understand.

Finally, communications breakdowns can lead to focusing on people rather than issues. These breakdowns can generally be attributed to one of three sources: (1) one side isn't listening; (2) one side has given up on the other; or (3) one side is formulating its next move. Listening is a difficult skill to master. But active listening will help enormously in sales negotiations. Use summaries and questions to check your understanding. One way to avoid giving up on the other side is to always turn the discussion on yourself. Instead of saying "you lied," use phrases like "I'm disappointed." Finally, to avoid formulating your next move while a customer is stating a position, work instead on understanding her position so you *can* formulate a next move.

Stating Positions

Once the positive climate has been established, you're ready to get into the meat of the negotiation—stating positions. This should be done by following the agenda established earlier. Generally, most sales negotiators feel it is best to handle pleasant issues first, controversial issues next, and neutral issues last. Most buyers will have some "hot button" that they will want to attack immediately. By holding them off for a bit, you stand a better chance of having them slow down and analyze their situation. A position should be stated by following these guidelines:

- State the interests first. For example: "Mr. Smith, you said at our last meeting that you were interested in

new technologies to keep your department competitive with outside firms—is that correct?"

- State the position. For example: "We feel that in order
to meet your objectives, a model 6600 with high-speed
graphics capability is the recommended machine."

- Provide proofs and rationals. For example: "We feel
that this model is the right one because of its high-
quality graphics, as demonstrated on this sample, and
because of the communications features which *Elec-
tronics Age* has called second to none."

Once the position is stated, you can begin the process of seeking
interests and alternatives.

Seeking Interests and Alternatives

Too often, we limit the effectiveness of negotiations by limiting
our alternatives. This is often a matter of perception. For example,
if I were to ask a group of people to compare two items—say,
automobiles—40% would probably list the similarities, 40% would
list the differences, and only 20% would list both. Unfortunately, it
has been my experience that sales representatives are more guilty
of this than almost anyone. After months or years of selling benefits, they are unwilling or unable to compare items in any other
light.

Yet it is critical to successful negotiations that alternatives be
sought often. By doing so, you *decrease* your natural desire to
"win" and *increase* the customer's openness. Here are some techniques that will help you seek alternatives:

- Be very specific in the statement of your position.
When discussing price, for example, include your costs
for production, warehousing, funds, and shipping.
This allows the customer to question more elements of
your position and possibly find alternatives. For example, if shipping costs are a major element of your
pricing, the customer may be able to take delivery at
regional rather then central locations.

- Seek comments on your positions. Phrases such as "Do
you agree?" or "How do you feel about that?" will get a
dialogue started.

- Talk futures—not pasts. Unlike the consultative approach, the negotiative approach does not seek to determine the *cause* of present problems but instead seeks the *purpose* served by the present supplier and whether or not those purposes match the customer's interests. The former looks backward to determine why a situation exists, while the latter looks forward for ways to improve. So instead of saying "I know you've been burned in the past by late deliveries," say "Our automated order entry system will improve delivery time by 25%." By taking this future orientation in your statements, you are automatically creating alternatives to which the customer must respond.

Summarizing and Closing

Finally, once a position has been explored fully and agreements have been reached, you can close on that position and move on to others. The close should include:

1. A summary of interests
2. An agreement that the interests have been served
3. A request to move on

When you have received these agreements, make note of them. It will probably be necessary to remind the customer of agreements later in the negotiations.

Closing a Sales Negotiation

Most, though not all (e.g., a temporary withdrawal), sales negotiations should end in a signed order or a specific action by the customer such as a study, or sample. If the negotiation has gone well, this action should be obvious to both you and the customer. Because you and he have stated your positions clearly and sought equally acceptable alternatives, the close should simply be a summary of the agreed upon terms and a question that asks for a specific action. Such "tricks" as the urgency or choice close should not be necessary since these issues have thoroughly been examined throughout the call.

Deadlocks

I wish I could assure you that every negotiation would work perfectly, if you only followed these directions. Unfortunately,

human beings are not as predictable as that. While you may follow
these techniques and have them work 99 times, on the 100th time,
you'll run into a buyer who, through stubbornness, stupidity, or
just plain meanness, blocks a settlement. What do you do? After all
this work, do you just walk away and try again?

Deadlocks are not uncommon in sales negotiations. As I said
earlier, there are more elements to a negotiation than just presenting the facts. Feelings, politics, and other pressures all have an
effect on the outcome of a negotiated sale. If you can (and I know
it's not easy), try to think of deadlocks as a natural stage of the
negotiation. If you don't go that far, at least try to regard them as a
challenge to overcome. But whatever you do, don't become discouraged because of a simple thing like a deadlock. You've worked
too hard planning and conducting the sales negotiation to let this
get you down. Here are five strategies that may help you overcome
a deadlock:

- The silent treatment. The silent treatment is appropriate in two instances: (1) where the customer has been
  very emotional and verbal in her defense of a position
  and (2) where your rationales may not be as firm as
  you'd like them to be. The silent treatment may force
  the buyer to talk herself into agreeing. The silent
  treatment works like this. If a customer has taken a
  position that you feel is unanswerable or inappropriate, calmly—but firmly—ask for an explanation. Then
  keep quite. Don't defend your position and don't develop a new position—just listen carefully to the response. Let the customer get it all out before you
  respond. You'd be amazed at how often the wind will
  come out of her sails.
- Temporary withdrawal. Often one of the best techniques to overcome a deadlock is to walk away from it
  for awhile. Let both sides catch their breath and think
  about how things are going. The key word here is
  temporary. It's easy for most sales representatives to
  engineer a temporary withdrawal. Simple phrases like
  "I have to check with my superiors" or "I'll have to see
  what the plant has to say about that" can serve to get
  you out of the negotiation for awhile. The temporary
  withdrawal is appropriate when you have made a lot of

concessions. In this situation, two purposes are served: (1) you are prevented from making further concessions and (2) the customer is made to think that he may have pushed you too far. Temporary withdrawal may also be appropriate if a single session has gone for a long time or if you really don't have firm foundations for many of your positions. In any event, the only firm rule of the temporary withdrawal strategy is to *establish a firm follow-up date*. Without a firm follow-up date, temporary withdrawal can very easily become unconditional surrender as you start to avoid the unpleasant experience of dealing with this buyer. You must hang in there to overcome any deadlock.

- Association is the third strategy for trying to overcome deadlocks. Association is a technique that attempts to relate agreement with a given position to higher goals such as prestige, security, "smart thinking," or personal advancement. The association technique is appropriate if the buyer seems insecure or when your position cannot be adequately defended in any other way. An example of association might be: "Stan, the most successful companies in town have all agreed that automated order entry is the way to go. Don't you think it's time you got on board?"

- Shifting is a technique that attempts to get the buyer to look at a position from another perspective. For example: "Instead of looking at it as a purchasing agent, let's look at it from the finance officer's viewpoint." You can try to shift the viewpoint to finance, marketing, manufacturing, executive, or any other function that relates to your product. It also works the other way. You can take the position of your warehouse management, or finance people, or even sales management to try and get the deadlock passed. "If I were the finance guys, and some sales rep asked me to allow that price, I not only wouldn't approve the price, I'd question his value to the organization." This is an example of shifting on your part. Shifting is appropriate when you find the negotiation becoming personal: in other words, when you find that either you or the buyer is becoming the issue, rather than the issues being discussed. By shifting, you take some of that attention away from the players and put it back where it belongs—on the interests. Be careful of one thing when using the shifting technique: avoid the "transparent salesperson syndrome." In this case, the sales representative tries to shift *blame* to others in the organization. For example: "I'd really love to give you that price, but the guys at the home office said no way." Transparent salesmanship never works and tends to end fruitful sales negotiations pretty quickly.

- The final technique for trying to break deadlocks is the piecemeal technique. In this technique, you try to get the buyer to agree to a small segment of your position and then come back to the position later on. This technique is appropriate when a buyer has been particularly adamant about defending a position. It's also a good technique to use when you have a really attractive offer to make "down the line."

The important thing to remember about deadlocks is that they are not necessarily a negative thing. Like an objection in a traditional sales role, deadlocks are signs that customers are still interested. Why else would they defend their positions so vehemently? So relax, sooner or later every deadlock is broken.

The Really Tough Customers

We talked earlier about the power bases of both the customer and the seller in sales negotiations. You may recall that I stated that your power emanated from the information you've been able to gather through sales calls, from the products and services you are representing, and from the ability to go to other customers to get business. You may also recall that I discussed the customer's primary power base as being the ability to call in additional suppliers. In the great majority of cases, I believe this will be the situation. But there are always a group of customers who defy the rules. These RTCs or "really tough customers," need not throw you into a panic. In most cases, they are representing accounts that have so much buying power that other suppliers are willing to make bad business decisions in order to get a share of the business. Or they may be buyers that have been buying these products or services so long that they actually know more about the business than you or most of your sales management. While this is not the ideal situation, there are ways to counteract it.

When you run into these types of customer, there should be two overriding considerations that rule your actions:

1.   Protect yourself against bad decisions.
2.   Expand upon your power bases.

It's very easy when dealing with large or prestigious accounts to lose track of what your purpose is in a sales negotiation. It's fairly simple to get carried away with having account X on the books or to be able to say to your boss: "I got the president of the trade association to do business with us." Neither of these are worth making a bad arrangement. So you should always have alternatives to doing business with this type of account. Alternatives might be *internal*—by that I mean lesser forms of business than you might normally pursue—or *external*—that is, other accounts that can provide the same volume without the time investment. When those alternatives are developed, keep them in mind during the negotiation. If it seems like you're going nowhere, exercise them and get out.

Power bases can be expanded in a number of ways. Clearly, the power bases you go in with are the most formidable. You are a recognized supplier, providing needed goods or services to the marketplace. That cannot be taken away from you. However, if you find yourself in a situation where these bases of power are simply not enough, try some of these:

- Find ways to inject information from activities you're carrying on at other accounts. If the RTC perceives that you are a valuable resource to *other* accounts, she may be less willing to "let you go" and may begin negotiating in good faith.
- Let the RTC know you're in the negotiation for the long haul and that you're not going to back down. Sure you need the sale but she needs suppliers. If she becomes aware that you're willing to work through negotiations for their long-term benefit, she'll probably be less willing to try to wear you down on minor points.

- When the going gets rough, appeal to higher ideals. Issues like fairness, for example, equal audience for all suppliers, good business practice like keeping options open, and precedents including agreements she has with other suppliers, will sometimes get the RTC off her high horse.
- Use rational argument and proof sources when the RTC starts making statements that can't be supported. Nine times out of ten you'll derail a "power trip" with this approach.

Really tough customers *are* difficult and not always worth pursuing. One of the most difficult decisions a good sales negotiator must make is when to pursue other opportunities. This is clearly a personal decision. Two months may be a lifetime for certain salespeople, while two years may just be the "warming-up" period for others. I'm sure you've been saying to yourself: "This is all great, but I don't think it'll work with my RTC." To that I can only say two things. Try it! Try some of these strategies before writing them off. And, second, don't be afraid to write off the customer. It's a big world out there. And there's lots of business to go around. There comes a time in negotiations when the best strategy is not to negotiate. Put the account on ice and get on with your career. This, however, should be the *absolute* last resort and one that comes only after long hard thought and continued attempts at success.

Summary

In our fast-moving economic environment, where technological advances, foreign competition, and ready venture capital can make products "commodities" almost overnight, solid sales negotiators are more than ever in demand. Overcoming what may be your natural distaste for this approach and dealing with the market in the way it wants to be dealt with may be your most important challenge in the coming years.

Sales negotiation is simply another way of giving customers what they want. If your company is successful, it is probably doing this in manufacturing, customer service, and other vital areas of its operation. Isn't it time that you, the "point man" in customer interactions, do the same?

6

THE ACCOUNT AFFILIATION MANAGER

Business-to-Business Affiliations

As our economy becomes more and more service oriented, buying decisions have had to change as well. Instead of simply buying products by the dozen, companies are increasingly looking to establish relationships with suppliers in order to maximize their purchasing power and add more efficiency to the purchasing function.

This phenomenon, of course, is not limited solely to the service sector. Even the most common commodity items must pass a specifications test before they're accepted. This too is a form of affiliation. Additionally, many manufacturers are adding service enhancements that require a long-term commitment. This is done to increase differentiation as well as establish long-term relationships.

Whatever the reasons, for many salespeople, selling cannot take place until a relationship has been established. Hence, the third role of the modern sales representative—the account affiliation manager. This role and those discussed in the next three chapters are strategic roles. By that I mean they relate to skills and knowledge necessary to plan and conduct sales campaigns. Account affiliation, relationship management, team selling, and prospecting may be required in either the consultative or negotiator environments. The skills required to complete a successful account affiliation are not limited solely to communications skills. Because of the scope of an affiliation, the successful account affiliation manager must be selling to the *right* people. He must also be able to assess a corporate culture and find a way to fit into that culture. Finally, account affiliation managers must have a pretty good understanding of human nature and organizational behavior in order to interact effectively with the various people who will be involved with an affiliation decision.

Whenever you sell something, you are acting as an agent of change. Even if the sale is a simple change of suppliers, change is taking place within the buying organization. In any change there are those who will welcome it and those who will oppose it. Factors such as convenience, comfort, security, relationships, and power enter into the decision to affiliate. This is true if you are asking an account to affiliate for the first time or to change from an existing supplier.

Differentiation and Momentum: The Engines of the Affiliation

Given this environment, the "sale" for the account affiliation manager is not so much one of presenting product benefits as lessening resistance to change. Many find this to be a much more difficult task.

In order to develop the strategies that will enhance your chances of successfully realizing change, it's important to understand two fundamental rules that most account affiliation managers follow:

- Change will not come unless there are significant positive differences between the current situation and what is being offered.
- Change gains or loses momentum based on the support of the people in the buying organization.

These two rules become the guiding philosophy for the account affiliation manager. She must be able to *differentiate* the product or service offered in order to maintain *momentum* with the organization's buying influences and decisionmakers. So let's take a closer look at these two rules.

Differentiation on the Market Level

How can a sales representative differentiate a product or service? Isn't that the work of marketing? While its true that companies spend millions trying to differentiate their products or services from the competition, differentiation at the account level or point of sale varies from the differentiation attempted at the broader market level in at least five significant ways:

- Differentiation on the market level requires mass communications. Differentiation on the account level is highly personal—often one on one.
- Differentiation on the market level concentrates on the broadest possible array of customer benefits. Differentiation on the account level concentrates on the sometimes narrow needs of individual buyers and influencers.
- Differentiation on the market level concentrates on the product. Differentiation on the account level concentrates on the person.
- Differentiation on the market level attempts to develop and sell an image. Differentiation on the account level seeks ways to demonstrate and deliver service capabilities.
- Differentiation on the market level attempts to *communicate* clearly the promises that a supplier will provide. Differentiation on the account level tries actually to *deliver* them.

To state it simply, the marketing department can differentiate on a broader set of issues and with the help of many different media. You have only one way to differentiate—through your own actions and behaviors.

In order to understand how you can differentiate yourself from the competition, it may serve us well to take another look at the customers involved in an affiliation decision. Once you've developed an understanding of who they are and what they're after, you may find it easier to position yourself effectively.

Three Unique Buying Perspectives

Almost any sale, other than those meant for immediate personal consumption, must appeal to a *constituency* of buyers. This is true whether the decision to buy is made by an individual or a committee; and it is certainly true of just about everything purchased in the business-to-business arena. These constituencies are made up of individuals who, like all individuals, have their personal quirks, likes, and dislikes. Yet because of their organizational position, they assume a role in the affiliation decision. These roles can broadly be divided into the following buying *perspectives:*

- Performance buyers. As was discussed at some length in Chapter 4, these are individuals who *use* or supervise the use of the product or service.
- Policy buyers. These are the individuals who influence an affiliation based on adherence to the current ways of doing things or against a set of previously stated specifications. They often have a technical background but may also come from such functions as personnel, budgeting, purchasing, or other policy-driven departments.
- Profit buyers. These are individuals who have access to the company's assets and can release funds. In many account affiliation situations, these people do not play a primary role until *after* the affiliation has been made.

One of your goals as the account affiliation manager is to differentiate yourself from the competition to as many of these constituent buyers as necessary. Each approaches the affiliation with a different agenda and it's up to you to try and satisfy them all. Will you succeed? Probably not. Why? Because as I said earlier, a lot of nonbusiness issues will likely surface in any account affiliation sale. Does that mean you shouldn't try? That's up to you. But I have yet to see any corporation or other business entity that required 100% agreement before a decision could be made. If you have taken all the right steps in trying to accommodate a given buyer and he still doesn't agree—then you'll have to start working on others so that momentum is maintained. In more cases than not, you will be able to realize the affiliation with or without some constituent members. So let's look at how you can differentiate yourself with these three buying perspectives.

Ten Ways to Differentiate Yourself with Performance Buyers

It is probably easiest to differentiate yourself with the *performance buyer*. Why? Because so few of your competitors will even bother talking to them. Chances are that they'll get so hung up in finding and developing "decisionmakers" that they'll lose sight of these people. Don't you do it! I have seen major deals for office automation equipment fall through at the last minute because nobody consulted the secretaries. Performance buyers are critical to the success of any affiliation strategy. You may be able to sign an agreement without them but I can almost guarantee it won't be worth the paper it's written on when it comes to implementation. Take the time to talk with performance buyers early in your affiliation strategy and it will pay dividends later. Here are some ways to differentiate yourself with performance buyers:

- Take a personal approach. Since these people's performance is often judged on the performance of your product or service, their perspective is often quite subjective. Use phrases like "What are your requirements . . . ?" or "What has your experience been with . . . ?" By getting performance buyers to state their preferences, you can begin to put together a strong performance story for other decisionmakers.
- Make sure your product knowledge is complete. Few performance buyers can resist a sales representative who actually sits down and operates a machine.
- Solicit specific "horror stories." Nothing will get a performance buyer talking faster than recounting past difficulties. A valuable side effect of these discussions is that they produce a firm basis for comparison between your offering and the current suppliers.
- Follow up sales calls in writing. These are often the forgotten people in affiliations. If you can show you listened and cared by writing a short summary note after the call, you've probably made a friend for life.
- Use demonstrations to back up claims. Often these are

the simple demonstrations rather than the ornate "dog and pony" shows reserved for more senior people. I once saw an office equipment sales rep make very big points with an office manager by proving that his 800 number answered faster than the competitions. Little things do mean a lot.

- Remain formal. Everybody calls a secretary by her first name. What better reason for you *not* to! If you need to make follow-up calls, set up an appointment. It will be greatly appreciated.

- Entertain the performance buyers. Your boss may have a problem with this but I guarantee you'll get a better return from a short lunch in the company cafeteria with a shop supervisor than you will from a five-course meal with a purchasing agent. And it will probably be more fun besides.

- Flatter performance buyers on their operation by making positive remarks on how well the department seems to be run or express awe at how they handle their various tasks.

- Demonstrate how your product or service will benefit them *personally*. Instead of drowning performance buyers in a sea of statistical information, show them how the product will make life easier. If you have reports that will save time and effort, take the time to show *how* it's an improvement over the current way of doing things.

- Ask if you can quote them. Make it known that you will be talking to various levels of the organization and ask if they'd mind if their comments were passed along to higher ups. Just be certain to assure them that you will be using their remarks in a positive way.

Ten Ways to Differentiate Yourself with Policy Buyers

Policy buyers are looking for something else from a sales representative. The primary responsibility of these people is to keep the company's options open and to restrict the possible excesses of management. Your natural inclination may be to regard these people negatively. Yet they do perform a vital function to the company. Control is essential to the success of any organization and as the saying goes, "Its a tough job but somebody has to do it." Instead of fighting it, accept it as just another step in the affiliation strategy. Here are some ways to differentiate yourself with the policy buyer:

- Solicit and familiarize yourself with current guidelines and procedures. The best way to get this information is simply to ask for it. By knowing what the guidelines are early in the sale, you'll have a better chance of aligning yourself with the policy buyers.

- Provide ways to measure any product or service claims you make. These buyers are concerned with quantifiable results and will rarely make a recommendation to affiliate based on subjective or "gut feelings." If you make claims for cost savings, provide ways to measure those savings or don't even bring it up.

- Seek their opinions. Often these buyers perceive themselves (or are perceived by others) as experts in their field. By playing up to those feelings, you not only differentiate but also may receive valuable information.

- Quote others in the buying organization. Because the function of many of these people cannot be said to contribute *directly* to sales or profits, many of them are highly "political" and have a heightened concern for the opinions of others in the organization.

- Determine the selection criteria used for present suppliers. Once you have determined what the existing criteria are, ask how they could be improved. By doing this, you not only may be able to influence criteria in your favor but may also cast some doubt on the wisdom of their past selection.

- Make all recommendations in writing I know you've already got enough paperwork to fill two lifetimes. But these buyers like to analyze proposals. By offering them ideas in writing, you operate in a way that makes them most comfortable. I'm not saying you have to make formal proposals every time you want to make a

point, but informal notes or summaries after a call will
help keep these characters on your side.

- Use demonstrations to quantify claims. If you think a
  demonstration will really prove a point, it's a good idea
  to use it. I wouldn't bother, however, demonstrating
  the "gee whiz" characteristics of your product. These
  buyers simply won't be very interested.

- Use referrals and third parties. Since these people are
  directed to maintain control, they often have a heightened interest in how others carry out this "thankless
  job."

- Use product literature liberally. Often these are the
  kind of people who never throw anything away. They
  pride themselves on knowing what's going on in the
  marketplace. So leave literature and follow up.

- Organize your calls on these buyers carefully. They
  will be favorably impressed if you have an agenda and
  stick to it. Chances are these buyers see a lot of salespeople; I'm sorry to say that being well organized will
  make you stand out from many of the others.

Five Ways to Differentiate Yourself with Profit Buyers

As I said earlier, in most cases, the *profit buyer* does not play a
major role in the affiliation until the later stages. These buyers
become important as you try to implement the affiliation agreement. Profit buyers, however, have to pass on the *need* for an
affiliation as well as some of the financial elements of the agreement. For this reason, it's important to know how you can differentiate yourself with these buyers. As I said, these are the people
who have access to the company's assets and can release funds.
Consequently, they are likely to be very bottom-line oriented.
Their needs are for firm documentation of savings or efficiencies
and they will want some sort of business case presentation. Here
are some strategies for differentiating yourself with these buyers:

- Demonstrate your knowledge of the organization and
  its needs. If possible, try to meet profit buyers later in
  the sales cycle, after you have held meetings with

performance and policy buyers. It's a pretty safe bet that these buyers are not in touch with their organizations on a day-to-day basis. By demonstrating that you are, you may be able to lessen the "accountant" mentality that some of these buyers bring to an affiliation proposal.

- Present price information in terms of costs not simply bottom-line numbers.
- Support claims with documentation and proofs. Provide examples of savings or efficiencies that others have realized.
- Make your presentations short and to the point. Provide written backup if you must but "net it out" for these buyers.
- Be analytical in your presentations. Note that your recommendations are being made after careful study and in keeping with the needs of the organization. Use graphic presentations whenever possible and summarize often.

Differentiation at the account level can often be accomplished simply by following some of these strategies. The other element of the affiliation strategy—momentum—is a little more difficult to control.

Maintaining Momentum Through the Sales Cycle

If you've ever tried to develop an account affiliation, you would probably agree with most of the sales representatives I've met that the most difficult thing to overcome is *lethargy*—not their own but the account's. How, they ask, do you get buyers excited when their perception is that things have never been better. It's this loss of momentum that most frustrates the account affiliation managers with whom I've worked.

Upon analysis, however, it's not hard to understand. Given what we know about change and how little real difference there is between products these days, it makes perfect sense that buyers will have a certain "here we go again" attitude toward new affiliations.

I think the point has been made that differentiation can be

controlled or at least influenced by the actions and behaviors of the sales representatives. But who controls momentum? Most of us would like to think the sales representative does. But is that really true? If you call a contact requesting a meeting and she replies, "I can't see you until next year" what happens to momentum? Its stalled. And that's the point. Momentum, in an account affiliation strategy, is controlled by the customers. How? By their decisionmaking. "Yes" decisions keep momentum going; "no" decisions stall it. Starting and maintaining momentum becomes an exercise in getting people to say "yes." No problem right? After all that's what they pay you for. But if change is as painful as we've said and differentiation is as difficult as it appears to be, to what exactly are they saying yes?

This goes to the heart of an effective account affiliation strategy—getting people to say yes to easy commitments or decisions. When regarded in its entirety, an account affiliation is an enormous commitment. Whoever says yes is committing the company to a relationship; and they're making that commitment practically blindly. No matter how they check references or look into your company's performance, the fact remains that those are past experiences and provide no guarantees for the future. Only the bravest businessperson is ever going to agree to make such a decision. If, however, others within the organization have expressed a need for change, then it's the constituency that's on the line. The risk is spread over a broader plane. If things don't go well, there are others to point the finger at. Developing an effective affiliation strategy is similar to running a bill through Congress. You must build a consensus for change among the various constituencies who will be affected by the affiliation. You build that consensus by putting a series of "easy yes" decisions before the various buyers and influencers. In order to give the strategy a structure, most account affiliation managers follow an orderly progression through the sale. You may develop your own system based on the requirements of your business. I'll offer a somewhat standard sales cycle that follows these five phases:

Phase 1   Contact. In this phase you introduce your company and its products or services, identify decisionmakers and buying influences, and establish the parameters of the affiliation.

Phase 2   Fact find. In this phase you define the current
           situation at the account and solicit dissatisfac-
           tions or concerns.
Phase 3   Present. In this phase you summarize the find-
           ings of the fact finding and contact phases and
           present your recommended solutions and
           affiliation terms.
Phase 4   Close. In this phase you seek agreements and
           commitments for action from all affected buyers
           and influencers.
Phase 5   Implement. In this phase you seek commit-
           ments to communicate and enforce the affilia-
           tion across the organization.

The process is cyclical in that once the implementation is established, contact is made with divisions, subsidiaries, or other
operating areas of the organization, and a complete cycle is followed with each of them.

If you accept this as a framework for an affiliation, the next step is
to provide yourself with a foundation for momentum. This is
accomplished by:

1.   Developing a series of "easy yeses" within each phase
      of the sales cycle.
2.   Assigning decision objectives to sales calls.

Keep in mind that what you are trying to accomplish in presenting an account affiliation is a major change in how the customer
operates. Since this is not an easy thing to do, it's important to
break down the affiliation proposal into smaller, more easily
accomplished pieces. Since decisions drive momentum, it's helpful
to discipline yourself to think in terms of the customer when
establishing the strategy. So, for example, instead of saying "I want
to get an appointment with Mr. Roberts by the end of the month,"
say "Mr. Roberts will agree to meet by August 30th." By using this
technique, you accomplish two things: (1) you train yourself to
think in terms of customer decisions *not* your own actions, and (2)
you provide yourself with a measurement of your progress after the
calls are completed.

The "easy yeses" for your product or service depend on what

goes into selling it. I have, however, been able to collect some fairly "generic easy yeses" that may help you to develop a strategy.

1. For the contact phase, the primary contact will agree to:
   a. meet with me;
   b. review literature and company background;
   c. accept the plan for researching the company;
   d. identify performance, policy, and profit buyers;
   e. communicate to these buyers that I will be contacting them;
   f. establish a timetable for communicating progress;
   g. review the findings;
   h. call a meeting of all interested parties to review proposals;
   i. assist in setting up meetings with hard-to-find contacts;
   j. provide straightforward feedback on all proposals.
2. For the fact find phase, *performance buyers* will agree to:
   a. describe the features of the current affiliation including relevant data such as price, delivery, service, operating procedures, and contact with vendor personnel;
   b. describe the *ideal* affiliation in terms of price, delivery, and so on;
   c. describe the conditions under which they would recommend a change.

   Policy buyers will agree to:
   a. describe the current strengths and weaknesses of policies relating to the affiliation;
   b. describe means by which policies could be changed or amended;
   c. pinpoint areas where the current affiliation is falling short of expectations.
3. For the present phase, appropriate buyers will agree to:
   a. attend a group session to present the terms and benefits of the affiliation;
   b. read proposals and ask questions by (*date*);

4. For the close phase, appropriate buyers will agree to:
    a. sign agreements;
    b. support the terms of the affiliation.
5. For the implementation phase, appropriate buyers
    will agree to:
    a. define the steps necessary to complete the affilia-
        tion;
    b. communicate the terms of the affiliation to all in-
        terested parties;
    c. provide lists of managers and profit buyers at all
        locations and/or departments.

This is only a partial list of the "easy yes" decisions you may wish
to put before customers. I'm sure that your business requires many
more specific agreements before an affiliation can be termed complete. The important thing here is to establish as many of the
commitments as possible *before* approaching the account. This
"anatomy" of a deal can be used over and over again in accounts
since the issues will usually be similar. When mapping your decisions keep these guidelines in mind:

- Make them measurable. Include dates for completion
  and specific outcomes.
- Make them action oriented. That's *customer* actions
  not your actions. Since the whole idea is to maintain
  momentum and momentum is derived from customer
  decisions, state your desired decisions in terms of *their*
  actions. Use verbs like agree, analyze, research, or
  sign.
- Make them reasonable. Keep in mind that the idea is
  to develop "*easy* yeses." If you think a decision is
  becoming complex, break it down into smaller parts.

Once you have developed all the decisions needed to complete
an affiliation, you can start assigning them to specific sales calls.
Clearly, any major account affiliation is not going to take place in
one or two calls. I have developed strategies with clients calling for
over 100 "easy yes" decisions. In that kind of situation, its very easy
to overload the buyer if you're not careful. Assigning a reasonable
number of decisions to a sales call becomes the vital link between
strategy and execution. For example, you may determine that on

the first call you can get your initial contact to review your literature, accept your research plan, identify performance, policy, and
profit buyers, and communicate to them that you will contact
them. Set those actions as your call objective. You can then plan
your consultative or negotiating call around those required decisions.

A Four-Tiered Approach to Measuring Your Progress

As you move through the sales cycle, it's important to keep track
of where you are. These are fairly complex strategies and you may
lose sight of your progress and become discouraged. Many account
affiliation managers track the results of each sales call in the affiliation strategy by using one of the following measurements:

> *Close*. In this outcome the customer has agreed to all re-
> quired decisions.
>
> *Progress*. In this outcome the customer has not fully agreed
> at the completion of a call but agrees to get back to you
> within a specified time frame. For example: "I'll check with
> my boss and get back to you by next Thursday."
>
> *Deferral*. In this outcome the customer puts you off without
> a firm follow-up. For example: "Let me think about it; I'll
> get back to you."
>
> *Refusal*. In this outcome, the customer refuses to make the
> desired decision(s).

By using this method of measuring your progress, you ensure
that you'll be aware of where you stand every step of the way. If
momentum is stalled because of deferral or refusal, you can take
immediate steps to rectify it without having to rethink the entire
strategy.

Presenting the Affiliation Proposal

Because the affiliation is generally long and rather involved,
there's a possibility that some of the buyers and influencers you
contacted earlier in the process will lose track of where you are as

time goes on. This can be dangerous, since you will, in all likelihood, need their cooperation to implement the affiliation after it's
"sold."

If at all possible, it's generally very valuable to try and bring the
buyers and influencers together for a group presentation. If you
can arrange it, you can accomplish a number of valuable objectives:

- You ensure that everyone is on board with the proposal. Periodic updates during the affiliation strategy
  are a good idea but often not feasible. By bringing all
  interested parties together for a meeting, you shake
  out some of the cobwebs.
- You are able to pit sponsors (those who support the
  affiliation) against detractors. I don't mean to say that
  the meeting should turn into a confrontation. But by
  carefully airing different positions within the organization you can at least demonstrate support.
- You are able to demonstrate the breadth of your research efforts to all interested parties. This is important because by demonstrating that you are willing to
  take time with the customer you increase *your*
  credibility and *their* openness to do business with you.
- If done well, the group presentation serves to simplify
  the affiliation strategy. By that I mean you can com-
  press all the terms and considerations into a half-hour
  presentation. As I said earlier, these affiliations are
  pretty risky business for the buyers, so anything you
  can do to simplify it can only help.
- Finally, the group presentation serves to solidify all
  the elements of the proposal in *your* mind. You're just
  as vulnerable to forgetfulness as the customers. By
  having to take the time to plan and present the proposal, you bring the entire strategy into clear focus.
  This not only will help you sell in the affiliation proposal but will also implement it.

Let's take a closer look at the group presentation from three
perspectives: (1) planning, (2) conducting, and (3) following up.

Planning a group presentation differs from planning a one-on-
one sales call. The major difference, of course, is the number of

people. When you are sitting in a customer's office discussing business, you pretty much have their undivided attention. In a group setting, that attention is far from guaranteed. A second major difference is that dialogue or give and take is limited. As we'll see later in this chapter, dialogue is not totally absent, but clearly you do not *want* the same level of dialogue that you would have in a one-on-one meeting. The presentation would quickly become a free-for-all. Finally, a group presentation generally has a time limit. While one-on-one sales calls may have similar limits, you can usually extend it if you're keeping the customer interested. So when planning group presentations, consider the following steps:

1. *Establish firm objectives.* As in most selling situations, it's the actions of the participants that matter most in a group presentation, not yours. So state your objectives in terms of the actions you wish the participants to take. For example: "As a result of this meeting, the participants will agree to read the proposal carefully and contact me with concerns or questions by next Thursday." An objective like this meets all the basic criteria for an effective objective. It is specific in terms of customer action, it has a time limit, and it is realistic in that it only asks that they review the proposal—not agree to the sale. This is a trap that may sales reps fall into. They think that they can get total agreement to an entire affiliation proposal as a result of one presentation. Usually, this is not the case. Your written proposal will probably have to be studied and analyzed before a go-ahead can be given. So set your objectives realistically. Don't look for total agreement; instead, gain agreements to study, analyze, or develop questions. The philosophy of "easy yeses" applies here as well.

2. *Set a time limit.* Different sales require different levels of presentation. However, such factors as boredom, hunger, and "fanny fatigue" are just as relevant for buyers of complex computer systems as they are for a housewife purchasing Tupperware. If at all possible, try to limit your presentation to 30–45

minutes. You must recall that, while you are very interested in what's being said, many of your participants may have heard it (and heard it, and heard it) before. Put long-winded or technical information in writing and include it with your written proposal. Be sure to allow enough time for interaction and questions and answers. If you have done the right things during the earlier phases of the affiliation strategy, the group presentation should serve primarily as a summing up and a statement of your proposal. Whatever you feel is the *minimum* amount of time you can allocate to this meeting should be established as your *maximum* actual schedule. You'll be surprised how you manage to get everything in.

3.   *Plan the opening.* As in the one-on-one call, there are a number of openings that can be effective. The tried and true general benefits statement can be successful. This is a statement of what's in it for the group. A statement of your agenda and objectives can also be valuable. A short outline agenda, in writing, is a valuable addition to this approach. Other account affiliation managers open their presentations with a question designed to gain people's attention. Whatever approach you choose, try to keep these guidelines in mind: (1) keep it short, (2) keep it simple, and (3) make it interesting.

The question of jokes often comes up when I'm running seminars on this subject. Are they appropriate? Do they establish the right climate? My view is—it depends. I have never been successful at delivering jokes and actually having people laugh. So I avoid them religiously. Others, however, have great success with humor and are really able to get people on their side in a hurry. If you feel you can pull it off, and if the audience seems, from past experiences, to be receptive, I say give it a shot. It really can break the ice.

4.   *Plan your questions.* As I said earlier, one of the great enemies of any group presenter is inattention. A

number of studies have been conducted on the attention spans of individuals in groups and none of them is very encouraging for people who have to make group presentations. Think about the last sales meeting you attended. Were you 100% attentive throughout the presentation? Probably not. I know that *your* presentation could never be considered boring but . . . Let's keep human nature in mind. One way to hold attention is through the use of questions.

Questions have a number of positive effects of group attention spans: (1) They introduce another voice into the presentation. This can be important if you have to speak for some time on a specific subject. (2) They create a certain accountability among the participants. They never know when they are going to be "called on" and hence increase their attention. (3) They allow others to make claims that might be questioned if you made them. (4) They act as effective bridges between major topics. (5) They can even gain information that was previously denied to you.

Group sales presentations are not training sessions, so it's important to use your questions judiciously. By that I mean if you are going to ask a participant a question, be absolutely certain she knows the answer. Don't overuse questions. Keep in mind that this is *your* presentation and the participants are expecting you to take charge. What kind of questions are most effective in a group sales presentation? Essentially there are five:

- *The Overhead Question.* This is a question directed at the group as a whole. For example: "Can anyone tell me how service calls are currently billed?" This question is appropriate in a number of situations: (1) when the information is easy and can probably be provided by almost anyone in the group; (2) when you are making a transition from one subject to another, for example, "Does anyone mind if we move on to the subject of pricing?"; and (3) anytime you feel you are losing the group's attention.
- *The Direct Question.* This is a question directed at a

specific member of the group. For example: "Steve, am I right that you feel maximum turnaround time on a special request should be 24 hours?" Direct questions are effective when you have a sponsor or champion in the group. These are people you know will support a position or proposition. They can serve to increase the credibility (and therefore the accessibility) of the individual asked and they can bring controversial information into the presentation without making you the bad guy. There are a few cautions, however, when using direct questions. (1) Always use the individuals name *first,* then pause, then ask the question. For example: "Mary, is my understanding correct—you would rather see cash refunds than credits to your account?" By using the name first and pausing for a brief moment, you ensure that the individual hears the question and is able to answer it. (2) Avoid controversial or philosophical questions. A question like "Tom, didn't you say you felt that the accounts payable situation was a mess?" may tend to make some people uncomfortable. (3) If possible, phrase these questions as closed end—yes or no type questions. Introducing questions with phrases like "Am I correct . . ." or "Did I understand you to say . . ." will take some of the heat off the respondent while still getting the reinforcement you need. (4) Finally, ask questions only in the individual's sphere of expertise. In other words, ask performance buyers performance questions, policy buyers policy questions, and profit buyers profit questions.

- *Hypothetical Questions.* These are questions, directed at the entire group, that do not require an answer. For example: "How do we ensure prompt delivery?" or "What are the terms of our warranty?" These questions are generally directed at specific features of your product or service and are followed by an explanation of a benefit. Hypothetical questions are valuable in making transitions from one subject to another. They are also valuable when dealing with difficult subject matter. For example: "Many customers ask me, 'How does the processor work?' " Knowing others have similar questions makes the participants feel better about their own doubts and uncertainties.

- *Reflective Questions.* These are questions that can get you out of tough jams. An example might be a customer asking you what the ideal delivery system is. Your reflective question would be: "What do *you* feel is the ideal schedule?" These questions should be used carefully so that you don't appear to be dodging the difficult subjects.
- *Restatement Questions.* These are questions that gain closure. For example: "If I'm hearing you right, you feel that the affiliation could be completed if we could provide departmental summaries on the management reports—is that right?"

The use of questions is a critical skill to effective group presentations and should be designed—at least partially—in advance. Think about your audience and how they will respond. Then outline a few key questions to keep yourself on track.

5. *Design visuals.* An essential means of gaining and maintaining attention in your presentation is to use visual aids to support major points. There have been many fine books written on the use and misuse of visuals and graphics in business. I am going to attempt to highlight some of the effective uses of visuals that I have seen account affiliation managers use in their presentations.

Visuals usually fall into one of three categories:

- Charts
- Graphs
- Prepackaged "shows"

Charts are visuals, usually consisting of text, that contain key points in abbreviated form. They highlight your presentation by reinforcing your words and giving the participants in the meeting something on which to focus. Some examples of charts include an agenda, a summary of major points, or even a closing question. Charts can be printed on flipcharts, posters, overhead transparencies, or other surfaces. *Graphs* are pictorial representations of information designed to make the information more accessible to the audience. Pie, line, or bar graphs are notable examples of this kind of visual. *Prepackaged shows* are professionally produced, canned presentations that have been created by marketing or public affairs to tell the company's story. They may be on film, videotape, slides, or slide–tape combinations like La Belle or Fairchild projectors. Each type has an appropriate time and place for use in group sales presentations and each can help you stand out from the competition. Here are a few tips for using them effectively:

- Try to prepare charts and graphs before the call.
- When using a flipchart:
  - Use black ink markers.
  - Leave 2–3 pages between each chart or graph to avoid "bleeding."
  - Write key points in pencil on the side of each chart or graph. This will be invisible to your audience but can act as a teleprompter for you.
  - "Index" the flipchart by placing small pieces of masking tape on each page you're using. Label the tape with a short, appropriate tab. This will help prevent fumbling around for the right page during the presentation.
- Limit pie chart segments to eight (8) to avoid clutter.
- Avoid opening a presentation with a prepackaged show.
- Avoid showing a prepackaged show for more than 5 minutes. This reduces the chances of losing your audience.

Conducting the Presentation

There are a few points you should consider when actually conducting the presentation. As you read, I'd like you to keep in mind the three *most* important factors that lead to successful sales presentations:

- Follow your plan. A group sales presentation with a sense of purpose and direction is a group sales presentation that works. You've taken the time to create a plan, now take the time to put it into action.
- Be yourself. A group sales presentation is not a show and you're not an actor. As long as you are following some of the basic principles we've been discussing—you can't go wrong.
- Don't panic. Whenever two or more people gather, no matter what the purpose, something unplanned will happen. Accept that as a fact of life.

Since you don't make presentations for a living, it's understandable that you may have trouble from time to time. Even the most experienced conference leaders sometimes find themselves caught up in an overhead projector cord or blocking a screen. Following these do's and don'ts will minimize potential problems and greatly increase your chances for a successful presentation:

DO

- Let your visuals do the talking for you on difficult subjects. Rather than explaining complex processes or analysis, create visuals that convey the information graphically.
- Maintain eye contact with the group.
- Breathe deeply before major points; this helps you to project the first lines' more forcefully.
- Stand to the left or right of a visual while writing on it.
- Establish a time limit and stick to it.

DON'T

- Read visuals. They're meant to support you, not act as a script.
- Confuse opinions with facts. Just because you feel an issue is important doesn't mean your audience does. On the other hand, the opinions of your buyers are a fact with which you have to deal.
- Be redundant. Statements like "sincere and heartfelt thanks" or "forward progress" are tedious and undermine your credibility.

DON'T

- Put your hands in your pockets.
- Leave the visual exposed after the point has been made. This tends to distract your audience as they focus on the visual more than on your words.

Closing the Affiliation Proposal

Your presentation should close with a call to action. Under the best of circumstances, the close is no more than a rephrasing of your objectives. You'll recall that I recommended that your objectives be stated in terms of the actions you wish the attendees to take. If you've followed some of the principles described here, you've given them the "whats and whys" of the proposal. Now is the time to get their commitment. Chances are they'll need some time to absorb what you've said before the decision can be made. Your close should then be specific actions that will help them in this thinking. Try these techniques when closing the affiliation presentation:

- Create a visual titled "Next Steps" or "Action Plan." Define specific actions required of the *group*, not you.
- Ask *each* participant if he's willing to carry out the steps that apply to him.
- Recommend specific time frames for each step's completion
- Offer your assistance on any step.
- Summarize.
- Open the meeting up to questions.

Keep in mind that throughout the affiliation strategy you've been closing on specific objectives in the plan. The final presentation is a time to remind buyers of actions they've already agreed to as well as getting them actually to move. You can afford to be a little "low key" and put the ball in their court.

Following Up the Presentation

It's not enough to leave the presentation and think your job is done. Unfortunately, human beings are pretty pathetic communication devices. Major points might have been missed, com-

mitments forgotten, or attention simply lost. Effective follow-up is
at least as important as the presentation itself. Unfortunately, in an
effort not to appear pushy or too hungry, many of us neglect this
important step. Here are some techniques effective account affiliation managers use:

- They write a short note to each participant immediately after the presentation. They thank them for
  attending and inform them that they will be contacted
  after they have had time to read the proposal.
- They telephone each participant after an appropriate
  length of time has passed.
- They prepare a list of questions for each participant.
  This encourages frank discussion and may provide a
  basis for changing the proposal.
- They provide summaries of other buyers' feelings to
  each participant. For example: "Joe in accounting feels
  that our management reports will be really helpful."
  This sort of summary makes each buyer think that a
  consensus is being built.
- They keep their key contact informed of all activity.
  This is the buyer who will keep the ball rolling, so it's
  critical that she remain on top of the proposal.

By thoroughly following up, you ensure not only that interest is
maintained but also that a line of communication is established for
the implementation that will follow a close.

Summary

Account affiliations are increasing all the time. Many buying
companies and institutions are joining together in co-ops and other
buying groups to streamline purchasing practices and realize more
clout with suppliers. Typically, these groups are looking to affiliate
with a limited number of vendors in order to leverage their
purchasing power against the widest possible range of products and
services. This is a unique opportunity to the salesperson who
understands how the process works and where he fits into the
overall scheme. At no other time in history has the efforts of the
salesperson been able to influence the flow of such large blocks of
business through his individual efforts.

7

THE RELATIONSHIP MANAGER

In most markets today, the great majority of business comes from existing accounts. In the medical field, we know where all the hospitals are and very few new ones are being added. In office products, large companies continue to provide most sales representatives with the bulk of their opportunities. The same can be said of the industrial, consumer products, and the service sectors. Indeed, many sales representatives are directed only at a select group of "key" or "national accounts," while smaller accounts are serviced by brokers, dealers, or manufacturer's reps. Yet in light of the overwhelming amount of business that comes from existing accounts, it's astounding how little formalized thought is given to maintaining and building relationships with this vital resource.

Whenever I've asked successful salespeople how they build and maintain profitable relationships with their major accounts, they make vague statements like "I service the hell out of them" or "I've established a good rapport with them." Very few can relate a definite plan or process that they use.

The fact is that *maintaining*, building and stabilizing business-to-business relationships, *is* the sale for many salespeople today. Often, no sales growth can be expected if the relationship between the supplying company and the buying company is not healthy.

Defining Relationship Management

Many salespeople make the mistake of thinking that their relationship with a single individual constitutes the entire relationship with the account. They speak of their rapport with the account and how solidly their "in" there. This view is, unfortuantely, dangerously naive.

As I've stated repeatedly, corporate buyers are influenced by a vast array of business conditions, constituencies, and concerns. To think that building a personal relationship with one buyer is enough to maintain stability in a vast business organization is like thinking that one account will provide enough volume to carry an entire territory. It *could* happen, but it's at best short-sighted and at worst disastrous.

What does the ideal account relationship look like? To some extent that depends on your business but see how you would answer the following statements on your best accounts. If you don't know, rate the statement false.

1. I'm considered *the* expert on my product at the account.   T F

2. I have *easy* access to every level of the account.   T F

3. I have done business with more than three contacts at the account.   T F

4. I can easily forecast who will support and who will oppose proposals I bring to the account.   T F

5. I am on a first-name basis with more than three people at the account.   T F

6. I am accorded "first refusal" on any competitive offers at the account.   T F

7. Account contacts often confer with me on matters that *don't* relate to my product.   T F

8. I understand how approvals are requested and granted at the account.   T F

9. I can get an appointment with my main contact in 48 hours or less.   T F

10. Most people at the account "volunteer" information (like staffing changes, reorganizations, and budget cuts) without being asked.   T F

Grade yourself using one point for every true answer. Apply these ratings to your responses.

9–10 Excellent

6–8   Fair

3–5   Weak

1–2   Poor

If you answered honestly and you're like most salespeople, you're relationships are probably weak to fair. The reason ratings are typically so low is simple: most salespeople spend an enormous amount of time selling product and virtually none working on the relationships.

To manage relationships you must examine *yourself* at least as closely as you examine your products and the competition. You are the "point man" in the relationship. Like it or not your customers are constantly observing, judging, and comparing your behavior to others. How are you measuring up? To find out consider these questions:

- What do accounts expect of you?
- How do accounts get things done?
- How can you position yourself to maximum advantage?

Buyer Expectations

I think most people (account personnel as well as salespeople) would agree that they want to remain in relationships that are essentially *stable*—not a lot of surprises or shocks. Most of us think of stability as a lack of change. Governments are considered stable when they don't change their system of government every time a general gets a bright idea. Companies are considered stable when they don't change management every time the stock goes down. But *is* stability really a lack of change?

Our constitution currently has 26 amendments—major changes to the law of the land made to maintain stability. Most of your major corporations, the blue chip, utterly stable foundations of our economy, would not be recognized by their founders. Consider your own relationships. If you've been married for awhile, is your spouse the same person you married? If your company were content to stay the same as it was when you joined it, would you be content to stay with it for a long time? Probably not.

This is the paradox of stability. In order for your account relationships to remain stable they must change. What kind of changes? Take a look at the sale from the buyer's perspective for a moment. Suppose *you* had to sit behind that desk for eight hours every day and *every* salesperson who came in pitched you on the same story. All you hear is how products will reduce costs, increase efficiencies, and improve profits. Wouldn't it all start to blur in your mind? Sure, your product may really *be* better, but unless you personally do something to demonstrate the difference, you're likely to become just another face in the crowd. Figure 7-1 illustrates how savvy buyers build up whole layers of expectations for the products they buy.

On the first level is the product itself. If you sell office supplies, your pencils should not break every time they're used, your staplers should not jam, and your paper clips shouldn't bend.

On the second level are the service expectations. These don't relate directly to the product, but it's pretty hard to imagine selling without them. Your deliveries should be prompt and contain minimal breakage, your billing should be accurate, and your terms should be reasonable. These requirements are expected and are a "given" in most sales.

The third level is the value added. This is the area where the successful relationship manager can excel. This layer consists of the *unexpected* things the salesperson can provide—true enhance-

Figure 7-1

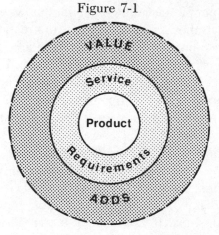

ments to the service offered. Continuing with our office supply example, value adds might include making recommendations for inventory levels, suggesting ways to improve requisitioning, and demonstrating automation processes.

Taking these factors into consideration, **relationship management** can be defined as *the process of maintaining and enhancing stability through the management of change.*

To be a successful relationship manager, you must be able to identify opportunities for changing the way buyers see you and your product and then manage a change in their operations.

By looking at your product in these three dimensions, you come to realize that what you are selling in major accounts is considerably more than goods or services. Every word you utter, action you take, or proposal you make has a ripple effect. If day in and day out the only thing you try to accomplish is the *expected*—you'll find yourself pigeon-holed as an everyday salesperson. Trying to sell-in new ideas, different procedures, or additional product is extremely difficult. Why? Because if you are an everyday salesperson doing the expected, trying something new becomes the *unexpected*. Customers are like anyone else: they don't like to be surprised. It concerns and frightens them; it makes them put up defenses, close their minds, and say no!

What if, instead, you made it your business to do the unexpected on every call. What if, every time you met with a customer you brought up new ideas, made daring proposals, or suggested different approaches to the business. What effect would that have on your account relationship?

It's human nature: your accounts would look forward to hearing from you. They'd know that a call from you wouldn't be just another ho-hum sales call. They'd look forward to discussing the business with you, banging around new ideas, or trying to solve problems. By taking this approach, you make the unexpected the *expected*. You add value to the relationship and become an actual resource to the account.

Am I suggesting that you develop these value-added proposals and ideas for purely cosmetic reasons? Certainly not. *Everything* you do should be directed at one simple objective—selling as much product or service as possible. Wasting valuable sales time on nonproductive activities like building rapport is not going to get you the things you want in account relationships.

So when formulating call objectives, you need to consider, in their order of importance:

1. What the proposal will do for *my* business.
2. What the proposal will do for the customer's business.
3. How the proposal will add value to the relationship.

Once you've determined how a proposal or idea will help you, the account, and the relationship, you need to consider how a business operates.

How Businesses Get Things Done

When I was starting out in sales, I thought of business institutions as the model of efficient, orderly organization. I envisioned nice, neat, chains of command with systematic procedures for making decisions. This naive 22-year-old thought that ideas and proposals were presented to the designated "decisionmaker" who reviewed the merits and approved or rejected them based on her predetermined authority level. If she couldn't approve it she "bucked" it up the ladder until it was approved or rejected.

I never really stopped to think about it, but I guess I pictured all the senior-level executives as just sitting around all day until a proposal came their way. Then they sit in judgment for awhile and stamp it yes or no.

It wasn't until I got my first headquarters job that I realized what *actually* happened. Most senior people are under so much pressure to produce, have so much desire to excel and stand out, that sitting around waiting for a proposal was about as likely as a shark swimming calmly around until a school of fish came its way. Depending on their personality, the power they had, and the unique agenda they were pushing, these so-called passive approvers would stick their nose into anybody's business. The real world of corporate decisionmaking is more like a volcanic eruption than an orderly planned process. Unlike the ladder of approvals I may have envisioned, the process is more like a pin cushion with all sorts of people sticking in ideas, agendas, and objectives.

In environments like this, simple decisions like purchasing office supplies can take on global proportions. An office supply is not simply an office supply but a *means* for improving productivity, realizing better returns on assets, increasing efficiency, securing competitiveness, enhancing resource management, and so on— depending on who's considering it.

While this, at first, may seem quite daunting, it's actually quite an opportunity. Think about it. Just about any benefit you stress on your product can probably find support *somewhere* in the account. Where in my old straight-line ladder theory of decisionmaking anyone in the chain of command could block an idea, in the pin cushion scenario no one can really block an idea because they're always reconsidering.

This doesn't mean that business is total chaos. Things *do* get done by following a prescribed decisionmaking process. In most cases that process looks like this:

1. A champion or champions proposes the change.
2. Interests and needs are examined with various interest groups and/or individuals.
3. Positions are developed.
4. Negotiation takes place.
5. A decision is made.

Champion Proposes a Change

A **champion** can be defined as anyone whose personal and professional goals coincide with your sales objective. In the best of all scenarios, a champion's goals are so intertwined with yours they become indistinguishable. But even if there is only partial sharing of goals, champions are critical to building productive relationships.

In many ways, the process is similar to tricks you may have pulled as a kid. Remember when you wanted something you knew your parents would immediately veto. One of the things you may have tried was enlisting the aid of brothers and sisters. You'd work on convincing your six-year-old sister that a motorcycle would really make her life better, while promising your nine-year-old brother endless rides for him and his friends. The hope was that such a groundswell of support would develop that your parents would see the proposal in a new light.

The account is like the family with one difference—you. You're an outsider. You're trying to influence this "family" in a way that will benefit you. Just as trying to sell a motorcycle to the father of four will probably not enjoy as much success as approaching the teenage son, so the decisions you propose to an account will require different champions.

In Chapter 6, I discussed at length the different *perspectives* that buyers have on a sale. If you have not read that chapter, it might be helpful to review it before continuing. The champion can come from any of the three perspectives developed in Chapter 6. *Performance buyers* may champion a change that will better their personal day-to-day experience. *Policy buyers* may champion a change that increases control, while *profit buyers* may champion a change that enhances the bottom line. Is there a *best* perspective from which to develop a champion? Careful analysis of the decision you're proposing will give you the answer.

Interests and Needs are Examined

It would be nice if every decision put before the account were analyzed only in the light of the benefits the company will receive—if only the "noise" of political and positional conflicts could be eliminated and a proposal could be reviewed in the clear sunlight of its merits.

But accounts are run by people and people have needs, concerns, and fears that can cloud the analysis of any proposal. So besides actual value of a given perspective, **interests and needs** are examined in light of two critical and interacting elements:

1. The *rate* of change
2. The *range* of the change

If you look at most of the "corporate miracles" of the last few years (like Lee Iaccoca's rescue of Chrysler, Walter Wriston's work at Citibank, or Gerald Tsai's work at American Can now Primerica), one thing stands out—the relative *speed* with which these miracles took place. Even though these men faced major hurdles in their quests, they had one advantage over you as a salesperson. Chrysler, American Can, and to a lesser extent The First National City Bank *knew* they were in trouble. Employees, managers, creditors, and suppliers were ready to change in order to save their skins. Your accounts may indeed *be* in trouble but they may not know it. And even if they do know it, they're probably not looking to you for solutions.

So the *rate* of change is a critical factor when considering a champion. Only certain individuals are capable of engineering rapid change within an organization.

What do Steven Jobs, Adam Osborne, and Donald Burr have in common? All three enjoyed enormous success at small entrepreneurial companies (Apple Computer, Osborne Computer, and People Express, respectively). Each also met his managerial demise when those companies grew. The *range* of change, that is, the number of people who are affected by what you propose, is the other critical factor to consider in champion selection. Like Jobs et al. there are some people who will be extremely effective at championing a proposal that affects a small number of people but virtually useless when larger numbers are affected. Conversely, others have no interest in small, limited exposure changes but will be enormously effective in the high-exposure arena of broad changes.

To visualize your proposal effectively, it helps to plot decisions on a grid as shown in Figure 7-2.

Each of the rate elements has unique characteristics.

A slow rate of change is usually characterized by:

- No clear plan—just a vague desire to change
- Lots of involvement from interested parties
- Lack of information
- Long-term/strategic outlook

Figure 7-2

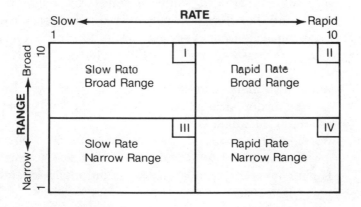

A rapid rate of change, on the other hand, is usually characterized by:

- A need for clear planning
- Little upfront involvement from the interested parties
- A powerful champion
- Lots of information (though not always enough time to
  analyze it well)
- Crisis mentality

Similarly, the range considerations also have unique characteristics.

Broad range changes are usually characterized by:

- Lots of resistance
- Stubborn resistance
- Often nonspecific, almost emotional, resistance
- Careful analysis
- Reluctance by the decisionmakers to act

Narrow range changes are usually characterized by:

- Minimal resistance
- Very personalized resistance (e.g., "Why me?")
- A "seat of the pants" approach
- Eagerness to act on the part of decisionmakers

As you'll see, these characteristics are important when it comes
to selecting a champion.

Let's take a look at an example of this system in action using a
product we're all familiar with—office supplies. Let's suppose, to
save shipping and handling costs, you wanted to change an
account's ordering cycle from every four weeks to every six weeks.

First, you need to ask yourself the three vital questions.

1. *What will the proposal mean to my business?* In-
    creased order size means less ordering and more
    profitable handling costs.
2. *What will the proposal mean to the customer's busi-
    ness?* Less order writing means lower labor costs.
    Higher inventory levels mean less out-of-stocks and
    fewer irate users.

3   *How will the proposal add value to our relationship?*
By offering labor-saving ideas the customer will begin
to see you as a resource they can depend on for
running their supplies business.

Based on these responses it would appear to be a "go."

You need to select a champion for this proposal. After all, it is a
change. They may have been ordering monthly for decades for all
you know.

So let's look at the rate and range aspects of the proposal. How
quickly does this proposal have to be implemented? Let's assume
your management wants to implement these new order cycles
within the next 12 months. In the supplies business that's considered pretty slow.

How about the range considerations? Well, the clerk who pre-
pares the order will have to change her habits. The supervisor who
approves it will have to make a change, and the accounts payable
clerk who pays the bill will notice something different. Three
people in one of your major accounts—no big deal.

You could plot the change on a grid like Figure 7-3. Based on
what you know about slow rate/narrow range changes, you can
anticipate no clear plan or position on the proposal, lack of information, minimal but personalized resistance, and a seat of the pants
approach.

How about another example. Suppose your company developed
an exclusive, new, longer-life typewriter ribbon—one that could
save the account thousands of dollars over time. There's one catch:

Figure 7-3

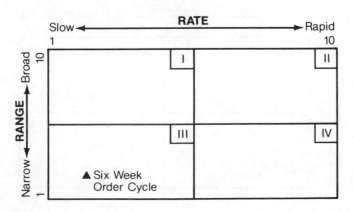

it isn't installed the same way as traditional typewriter ribbons. Every secretary will have to take a short, five-minute course to learn the new installation procedures. Your company is a little hesitant on the product and has said you must sell it in the next three months or they'll withdraw it.

First, ask the three vital questions:

1. *What will the proposal do for my business?* Because it's an exclusive, your competition can't move in. You stand to gain an enormous share in the ribbon category.

2. *What will the proposal do for the customer's business?* Because of its longer life, replacements won't be required as often; the account will save money and time as fewer orders are processed.

3. *How will the relationship be improved?* By offering new technology and money-saving ideas, you'll establish yourself as a major resource in office supplies.

Based on these answers it seems to be a solid proposal. How does it stack up on the rate and range grid? Your company has given you three months in which to sell it. In the supplies business, three months on a new product is considered rapid. On the range side, *every* secretary is going to be re-trained. That's hundreds of people and can be considered pretty broad. This proposal would be plotted as in Figure 7-4.

Based on what you know about rapid rate/broad range changes,

Figure 7-4

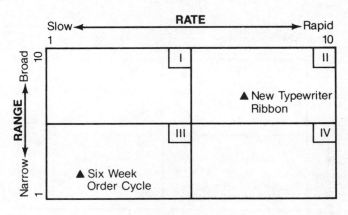

you can expect a need for clear planning, well thought out response to the proposal, crisis mentality, and lots of resistance, emotionalism and reluctance to take a stand.

Clearly, the second decision is going to require a totally different type of champion than the first. To begin to understand the characteristics of these different champions, it's helpful to understand how positions are developed.

Positions Are Developed

In most cases, **positions** are developed in relation to the effect the decision will have on two factors—*perspective* and *power*. You've seen the perspective dynamic at work in your own organization. Sales wants to lower prices in order to meet competition; manufacturing says no way. Finance is skeptical on the effects a reduction will have in earnings and marketing sees a possibility of tarnishing the product's image. In the best of all worlds, perspective would be the only "factor" considered in corporate decisions. After all, each perspective has a legitimate concern for its own well-being and that concern is generally good for the organization as a whole. In the real world, however, other concerns surface. These are *power* concerns and nothing can disrupt a relationship more than being insensitive to power needs.

It may help to begin with some sort of definition of power. When conducting seminars on this subject, I often ask participants to define power as they see it. Answers vary, but generally fall into one of the following categories:

1. Power is the ability to get things done.
2. Power is the ability to impose your will on others.
3. Power is strength.
4. Power is something you have that others lack.
5. Power is the decisionmaking ability.

These are all pretty good answers but they have a common flaw. They regard power only as a *positive* thing. They regard it only in the global sense as in the power of kings, dictators, or other absolute rulers. Is this the reality of today's business environments? Like the political arena, the business arena is an intricate maze of influences, constituencies, and interest groups. It's very difficult to find any single individual who has absolute power over a business enterprise. One only has to look as far as the recent fate of Steven Jobs at Apple Computer to know that power can be denied even to the founder.

To understand and leverage power, it's important to realize that power has two levels:

- The power to say yes. This power is usually limited to a handful of people who can actually release funds or set policy.
- The power to say no. This power generally has a broader base, extending at times to very low levels of the organization.

It would be a serious mistake to think that you can make change happen only by concentrating on those with yes power. Relationship management is at least as concerned with avoiding "nos" as it is in *securing* "yeses."

The Four Power Bases

Relationships are managed by covering all the power bases in the buying organization. What are the power bases? There have been a number of studies conducted on organizational power and an equal number of theories put forth. I'd like to limit our discussion of power to four types:

- Reward power. This is the power to provide monetary, psychological, social, or political benefits to other members of the organization. This might include salary increases or bonuses, increased sense of security or belonging, closer social ties, or increased organizational exposure.
- Attraction power. This is the power to persuade based on some attraction an individual has with others. While it may be actual physical attractiveness, it more likely relates to perceptions that an individual is "on the move" or well liked by those with reward power. The basis of this power is in the desire to emulate the empowered individual and therefore go along with his position.

- Expert power. This is the power that emanates from some real or perceived expertise that an individual possesses. It may be derived from first-hand knowledge of an operation, technical knowledge, or educational background (e.g., an engineering degree).
- Status power. This is the power that emanates from organizational position. Vice presidents generally have more of this power than directors, who in turn have more of it than managers and so on.

It's important to remember that with any of these power bases, the power does not necessarily have to be exercised to ensure compliance with a decision. For example, the individual with reward power does not have to give out bonuses every time a decision is placed before the organization. The simple fact that she has the power and is supportive of the change should be enough. Additionally, one person may have more than one power base. An expert can also have status. Attraction power can be coupled with reward power, and so on.

The Strengths and Limitations of Power
Each power base has strengths and limitations. Understanding them will help you leverage the power base more effectively.

- Reward. This power base can be very effective in a variety of situations. Once this individual has "blessed" an idea, it remains "blessed" until the individual alters her position. This is not always true of the other power bases. It is also a very efficient power base, because it reduces the need for negotiation and red tape. On the negative side, this power base is heavily dependent on the individual. If she goes, so does the power base. It also creates the opportunity for resentments if other members of the organization are "steam rolled."
- Attraction. This power base is a very dynamic one. People respond to these individuals in an almost emotional way and often neglect careful analysis. It is generally the easiest power base to leverage because of the ego aspects associated with it. These individuals

generally are more receptive to change—seeing it as an opportunity to "look good." On the negative side, this power base can be somewhat ephemeral. If the individual loses face—even once—the power base begins to deteriorate. Additionally, the universality of this power base is questionable. There is a possibility that a certain amount of petty jealousy, resentment, and hostility will be at work undermining attraction power.

- Expert. This power base can be very powerful. Some experts achieve almost "guru" status in the organization and others are very reluctant to oppose them. These individuals are generally open to new ideas and innovations as a means of solidifying or furthering their expertise. The power base is limited, however, by strong egos. These individuals are very reluctant to change a previously supported position in fear of losing their "guru" status. Additionally, their power may be limited to a small portion of the overall decision.

- Status. The status power base is fairly stable and tends to live on regardless of who holds the office. These individuals have *functional* responsibilities (such as accounting, finance, or sales) and therefore the decision can be phrased in those functional terms.

Clearly, certain power bases are more appropriate for certain decisions than others. As we'll see, an understanding of these dynamics is crucial to the selection of a champion to guide you through the organization.

Relating Power to the Proposal

To determine which power bases are needed to make a proposal work, take another look at the decision grid (Figure 7-5) we developed earlier. Different power bases relate positively and negatively to different quadrants.

Quadrant 1—Slow rate/broad range

- Reward power. Reward power is an appropriate power for a champion to have because of the broad resistance this type of decision is likely to encounter. Reward power may be the most effective power in lessening

Figure 7-5.

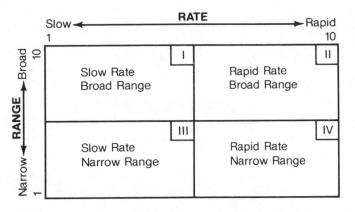

that resistance and clearing the way for the decision.

- Attraction power. This power base is *inappropriate* for the same reason that the reward power is appropriate. It is a rare individual who has attraction power across a wide spectrum of the organization.

- Status power. This power base is probably effective because the resistors have to respect organizational power. Be aware, however, that these individuals are probably conservative in the use of their power in order to protect their status. The fact that this decision has a slow rate works well in light of that fact.

- Expert power. Unless the decision is of a highly technical nature, it's unlikely that people with expert power can influence a broad range of the organization.

Quadrant 2—Rapid rate/broad range

- Reward power. Because this is the most far-reaching and controversial of the decisions, having reward power assists your champion greatly.

- Attraction power. This power base could be effective owing to the crisis mentality of this kind of change. It also gives the person with attraction power the ability to "strut his stuff."

- Status power. This is probably inappropriate because of the inherent conservatism of this group. Rapid change is controversial and they would probably just as soon avoid it.

- Expert power. This power base is probably in-appropriate because of their penchant for careful study and review.

Quadrant 3—Slow rate/narrow range

- Reward power. This base is probably inappropriate because of the global perspective of these individuals. They probably do not want to get involved with the level of detail that these decisions require.
- Attraction power. This base is probably inappropriate because of the limited results inherent in the change. These individuals usually want to make a bigger splash.
- Status power. This may be the most appropriate power base for a champion in this kind of decision. Slow, well-planned change allows these individuals to retain the integrity of their position.
- Expert power. This power base is also highly suited to this kind of decision. The expert is allowed to analyze the decision carefully and to protect his "guru" status.

Quadrant 4—Rapid rate/narrow range

- Reward power. This power base is appropriate because of their ability to get things done quickly.
- Attraction power. This power base is appropriate be-cause of the opportunity to gain prominence quickly.
- Status power. This power base may be appropriate because of the narrowness of the risk exposure but be aware that these individuals may be reluctant to move that quickly.
- Expert power. Rapid rates of change make people with this power base nervous but they may be willing to champion it because of the limited exposure.

Negotiation Takes Place

The *negotiation* phase of the decisionmaking process is the most volatile and for you, the seller, the most frustrating of the phases. It's frustrating because of your inability to take an active part in the process and it's volatile because all the power and perspective factors come together—sometimes in explosive combination.

Here's how it works. Generally, an account establishes some formal or informal system for concurrence. Chances are your company has a similar system at headquarters. Affected parties can concur or nonconcur based on their own interests. The decision works its way through the organization until all parties have been heard. Changes are made to the initial proposal based on the input from the interested parties.

A Decision Is Made

The *decision is made* when at least a majority of the interested parties see value in the proposal or when one of the power bases imposes the change. This process may take days or months depending on what you are proposing.

Positioning Yourself to Maximum Advantage

Successful relationship managers determine their role in the account based on the realities of the decisionmaking process. Rather than fight the process, they *leverage* it by positioning themselves with the right people in the account. This involves:

- Determining changes that will provide value-added benefits to the account and developing a proposal (formal or informal).
- Forecasting the rate and range effects of the decision.
- Selecting and developing a champion.
- Determining what perspective, power, and personality forces will be needed to get the job done.

Let's examine each step more closely.

Determining Value-Added Changes

An effective way to begin this first step is to take a few hours and thoroughly analyze your accounts. What can *you* do that your competition either can't or doesn't do? You know what they have to offer and you probably have a pretty good idea of how effective they are at offering it. Start by listing all the things you currently do. This should include both product and service requirements.

Next, take a close look at the account's operation. Are there inefficiencies, waste, or other problems that could provide opportunities for you to shine? If you've done a thorough analysis, you'll probably develop quite a list. Establish priorities based on the value each will have on the relationship. Consider the three vital questions:

1. What will the proposal do for my business?
2. What will the proposal do for the customer's business?
3. How will the proposal affect the relationship?

Choose the best proposals and go on to the next step.

Forecasting the Rate and Range Effects of the Decision

Take a close look at what you're proposing. Ask yourself: "How quickly do I want the account to implement this change?" The answer will depend on your business. If it usually takes six months to get a decision implemented and you want this to happen in three, call it rapid. If it normally takes six months and you think it's reasonable to accomplish this in nine, call it slow.

Then ask yourself: "How many people will be affected by this change?" Are major portions of the organization going to have to concur on this proposal. If so, call it broad. If only a department or two will be affected, call it narrow.

Plot the proposals on a decision grid as in Figure 7-6.

Figure 7-7, a planning guide, should help.

Figure 7-6

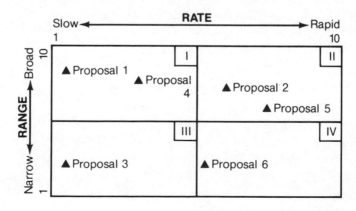

Figure 7-7

Account Analysis Planning Guide

Contact	Perspective	Power

Selecting and Developing a Champion

To select a champion you need merely cross reference:

- The rate and range quadrant into which your proposal falls.
- The appropriate power and personality types for that quadrant.
- The person or persons who, based on your analysis, best fit the bill. Use the quick reference guide, Figure 7-8, to help you in this selection.

Is the *selection* of a champion the only consideration with which you should be concerned? Will the champion (even the right one) do your job for you? Unless you're the most persuasive sales rep in the world, the answer to both those questions is probably—no!

To *develop* the champion fully, you have to map out the decision and clear the way for action. Decision mapping involves:

1. Identifying influencers and decisionmakers.
2. Determining and providing for *their* information needs.
3. Anticipating and answering *their* objections.
4. Seeking *their* commitments.

Determining What Will Be Needed to Get the Job Done

If you can, this map should be developed with the champion so that you are in step when it comes to running the decision through the business. Let's take a closer look at the decision map:

Figure 7-8

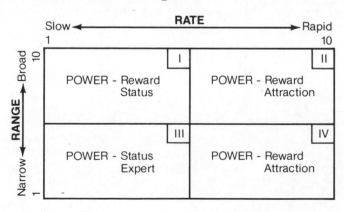

1. Identifying influencers and decisionmakers. You'll re-call earlier that I spoke of power in terms of two levels: the ability to say yes and the ability to say no. Most relationship managers define decisionmakers as those with the ability to say yes and influencers as those with the ability to say no. Influencers should be identified along both perspective and power tracks.
2. Determining and providing for information needs in-volve selling benefits to each unique perspective. As I said earlier, the performance buyer is concerned with operations, service, ease of use, and other everyday needs. The policy buyer is concerned with controls, policies, and procedures, and the profit buyer is con-cerned with the bottom line. The champion should be armed with this information before she starts running the proposal through the business.
3. Objections are predictable, up to a point, based on the rate and range considerations you're proposing. They'll also generally follow both perspective and power lines. Based on what you know about per-spective, those objections should be fairly easy to anticipate and discuss with the champion. Power objections, more personal and difficult to address, are also more difficult to anticipate. Below are some objections you might anticipate from each of the power bases.

*   Reward. Objections will often center around changes to the makeup of the organization and the effect of the change on certain individuals. Reward power is gener-ally very broad-based and the wish to protect that base is of primary concern. Additionally, these individuals may wish to know costs and expenses associated with the change.
*   Attraction. Objections from this power base will gener-ally relate to personal risk and image considerations. These people may be cautious at first as they attempt to assess the personal ramifications of a decision.
*   Status. Objections will likely relate to effect on the status quo and larger organizational issues.
*   Expert. Objections will probably relate specifically to

the product or service or to other technical factors within the company's operations (e.g., network compatibility with a new telecommunications equipment).

4. Commitments can be major—like signing a purchase order—or minor—like agreeing not to block a study. They should be identified and stated as objectives with the champion.

Let's follow the office supplies scenario through the entire process.

Suppose you are selling office supplies to a major corporation. You currently enjoy 33% of the business and you would like to increase that to 45%. You've analyzed the account and have determined that a requisition system for office supplies would help the account get a handle on costs. Since your automated billing system can be tied directly to such a system, you feel you can gain a real value-added advantage over your competition. You've determined that it should take seven months to implement this system, which is relatively slow. It will affect nearly the entire organization, however. You've plotted the proposal on the rate/range grid as in Figure 7-9.

The account has five key contacts and influencers. First, there's Joe Morgan, the purchasing agent. Joe's a timid fellow who doesn't like to rock the boat. He knows his stuff when it comes to negotiating a deal but he has very little vision beyond his own function.

Figure 7-9

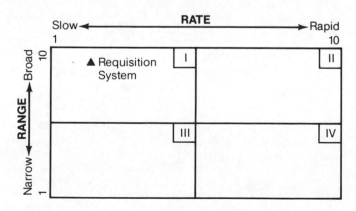

He'll get excited about saving $1.50 on a gross of paper clips but bring up real cost savings like productivity, efficiency, or resource management and his eyes glass over.

Mary Simmons is the Director of Office Services. She's a pretty hard-driving individual who's really concerned with things like productivity and workloads. Mary's recognized as someone on the move and people generally sit up and take notice when she speaks. She's been able to save the company a lot of money by making intelligent purchases at the right time.

Tom Mullen is the Director of Corporate Policies. You don't really know him very well but he seems kind of aloof and distant. You're feeling is that he'll probably go with the majority on this one. He's got bigger fish to fry and he doesn't really understand the business.

Lenore May is the Controller. She's very intelligent and well respected in the organization. Lenore is very analytical, has the power to move careers along, and wants to get ahead. She's been interested in proposals you've made in the past and she has a reputation for getting things done.

Charles Young is Lenore's boss. He rarely gets involved in decisions relating to office supplies. Charles has the ability to stop anything that either Joe, Mary, Tom, or Lenore cook up. But you feel in this decision he'll probably just "rubber stamp" whatever they come up with.

You've analyzed the account and made up a planning guide as in Figure 7-10. Since the proposal falls into quadrant I (slow rate/ broad range), you know that the reaction will be characterized by no clear plan, lots of involvement from interested parties, stubborn, emotional resistance, and careful analysis. You also know you'll need either status or reward power to get it done. Since policy is going to be changed and profits affected, you realize you'll need one or both of these perspectives to run the proposal through the business.

As you review the planning guide, you'll see that three people are possible champions for this proposal:

1. Lenore May
2. Tom Mullen
3. Charles Young

Figure 7-10

Account Analysis Planning Guide

Contact	Perspective	Power
Joe Morgan (Purchasing agent)	performance	expert
Mary Simmons (Dir, office services)	performance	attraction expert
Tom Mullen (Dir, corp. policy)	policy	reward
Lenore May (comptroller)	policy, profit	reward
Charles Young (Treasurer)	profit	status

Mullen and Young have never shown much interest in office supplies and besides they only bring one of the perspectives to the decision. The logical choice is Lenore. Her power and perspective are matches to those required by the decision and she has expressed interest in past proposals.

To map out the decision for Lenore, you'd consider her perspective and power base. After making an appointment, your first call might look like this:

You:	Ms. May, I'm John Troy from Amalgamated Office Supplies. We've been doing business with your company for a number of years. I've been studying your operation and I think I've come up with a way to save considerable amounts of money in managing office supplies. Would you be interested in investigating this?
Lenore:	Sure.
You:	In reviewing your supply room, I noticed that there's no real system for ordering and distributing supplies. Anyone can pretty much take whatever he likes. How do you feel about that?
Lenore:	Frankly, it's a little embarrassing. We should have tighter controls. What did you have in mind?
You:	We've had a lot of success with installing a requisition system at accounts like yours. It involves developing a standard form like this, which must be completed for every order.
Lenore:	Interesting.
You:	The beauty of the system is that it can tie directly into our automated order system, so that you receive a computerized statement of user levels by department.
Lenore:	That's very impressive but I'm not sure I can really find the time to make it happen. Besides, maybe you should be talking to Office Services.

You:	I'd be happy to speak with anyone you feel is important in this kind of a decision. How would you go about getting a decision like this made?
Lenore:	Well, I'd have to make a pretty strong case with Charlie Young, our Treasurer. That shouldn't be a problem though. Then we'd have to get Mary Simmons on board.
You:	How would you go about that?
Lenore:	She'd be concerned with the productivity of the supply room, how much time the system would take, personnel levels—things like that.
You:	I could provide statistics we've developed with other accounts that demonstrate that a system like this has virtually no impact on productivity. In fact, it can help it.
Lenore:	Why don't you send it over.
You:	Glad to. What else would be involved?
Lenore:	Tom Mullen would want to be aware of this. He controls our policies and would want to write a specific procedure.
You:	I have examples of procedures we've developed for other companies. That should make his job a lot easier.
Lenore:	The biggest problem would be with Joe Morgan in Purchasing. He'd have to review your departmental report before every purchase. He'd probably have a problem with that.
You:	I know Joe pretty well. If you pointed out the cost advantages to him, I'm sure he'd cooperate.
Lenore:	All the department heads would have to be notified. Tom can handle that. The secretaries would have to be trained.
You:	We have some really good samples of training pieces. It won't be a problem.

Lenore: It really isn't such a big deal. Is it?

You: Not really. If you get behind it, it could be handled very efficiently. Could I ask you to get clearance with Mr. Young, and then set up a meeting with yourself, Ms. Simmons, and me?

Lenore: Sure. I'm meeting with him this afternoon. Call me tomorrow and I'll set things up.

The interesting thing about this way of selling is that the precall analysis really pays off. Because you're speaking with a person who has the ability to get the job done, you're not dealing with a lot of foot dragging and hemming and hawing. Often, you'll be surprised at the reception you get and how quickly action is taken.

Managing Relationship Campaigns

A question that often comes up is how *many* decisions should be put before the organization in a given time frame (e.g., a year).

This is a judgment call to a certain extent, but some guidelines can be provided.

1. Develop one major decision at a time. A multifront assault will make you seem like a nuisance.
2. Allow the dust to settle after a decision has been made in your favor. The time frame depends on your business but generally the recommendation is at least two months.
3. Follow rapid-rate changes with slow-rate changes and broad-range changes with narrow-range changes.
4. Try to alternate champions with each decision.
5. Be sure that the last change is fully in place before suggesting another.
6. Try to avoid using people affected in a prior change as champions in a subsequent change.
7. Try to have every perspective and power base champion make at least one decision per year.
8. Don't be reluctant to let the account rest for awhile. Too much activity is *almost* as bad as too little.

9. Keep records of the most vocal resisters to a given decision, then try to use them as champions the next time around.
10. *Never* develop a proposal without satisfactorily answering the three vital questions.

Summary

No single proposal will establish a solid relationship with an account. But think about the aggregate of two, three, or five years of taking this approach. How well established would you be if every level of the organization had some sort of interaction with you.

The nice thing about building relationships this way is that it's painless: clearly painless to you because you're developing the account, but painless to the account as well because you're giving people the opportunity to exercise their power and influence for the good of the company.

With all these things going for it, it's surprising that more salespeople don't take a more planned approach to relationship management.

8

The Team Seller

As technology becomes more and more complex and services become of equal or greater importance than products themselves, the need to involve others in the sales process is increasing. Examples of industries that require nonsalespeople to interact directly or indirectly with customers abound. Data processing and telecommunications companies must deploy systems engineers, trainers, and installers to help make the sale. Service companies like travel agents, security firms, and transportation services must entrust elements of the sale to such functions as service coordinators, traffic, or quality control. Even law and accounting firms, consultants, and advertising agencies must parade their experts before the client if they hope to get the business.

This situation presents some unique opportunities to sellers but also poses potential difficulties. On the positive side, tremendous synergies can evolve between your people and theirs. It's efficient. Rather than have you gather mountains of information that you may or may not fully understand, team members can cut through the "corporatese" and get to the fundamentals quickly. On the negative side, there can be dangers. Claims made on earlier calls may not be properly reinforced if others on the sales team are not properly coached. Contradictions can arise if presentations are not carefully planned. And the customer can become confused if you're not presenting a united front.

For these reasons, the challenge in team selling is a *management* challenge even though you, as team leader, are probably not functionally a manager. As team leader, you have to ensure that your resources are being used efficiently and for maximum payoff. To accomplish this management objective, it's important to:

139

- Allocate time and people effectively
- Master the secrets of successful group dynamics
- Keep informed through reporting and control systems

Let's look at each element in more detail.

Allocate Time and People Effectively

Its been my experience that one of the most difficult things for the team seller to overcome is his own ego. Effective team sellers recognize that they are also team *members*, that their role is no more or less important than any other team member to the successful completion of the sale. The reason some have this difficulty is easy to understand. They are usually the team leader and as such have the greatest exposure to the customer base. Chances are they are the only team members who possess any understanding of sales and the sales environment. They express frustration when other team members don't communicate well or to take the customer's side in difficult situations. To overcome these frustrations, team sellers must be able to recognize who is necessary and how much time is necessary to make the sale and then allocate and control those resources effectively. Resource planning involves:

- Establishing a sales plan
- Creating objectives for each phase of the plan
- Allocating the time resources appropriately

Establishing a Sales Plan

I've discussed *sales plans* in depth in Chapter 6. Most sales plans follow a more or less standard cycle. In Chapter 6, I established a standard cycle that included contact, fact finding, presenting, closing, and implementing. Your cycle may include additional phases depending on the requirements of your business. What's different about team selling situations is that you will not be able to complete some or all of the phases without help. The sales plan becomes the document from which you enlist help from the other team members. As we'll see later in this chapter, team members respond well when they feel that there is a firm plan. Some team sellers enlist the aid of the other team members in drafting the sales plan. Should you? In most cases I would not recommend it. There will be ample time to build team spirit and commitment during the sales campaign. By drafting the preliminary plan your- self, you are communicating that you are in charge to the other team members. You are also saying to them that you are the salesperson and you can handle the sales chores. When putting the sales plan together keep these guidelines in mind:

- Keep it flexible. Don't try to overplan by committing people to very specific dates and times. A range of three or four days will not usually hold you back.
- Don't request *specific* people this early in the cam- paign. If you need an engineer, simply note that need. Don't insist on the best engineer at this point.
- Keep it neat. Try to have the plan typed or at least neatly printed. A good-looking document demon- strates that you have worked hard and increases the commitment of the other team members.
- Be sensitive to the concerns of other team members. Try to use their language when developing the plan. Avoid sales jargon. Team members will be more will- ing to accept your plan when they understand it.
- Use proposal type language such as "recommended" or "submit" rather than authoritative language like "re- quired" or "demanded." This will give team members the impression that you are open to suggestion on the plan.

Creating Objectives

As in the account affiliation plan, once the phases are es- tablished, you can begin to build in "easy yes" decisions and establish them as call objectives. This is the point where you will need to determine who does what in the plan. If the decision you need requires technical support to even ask the right questions, you must be able to assign the right technical person to that objective. By establishing the objectives upfront like this, you also create a communication mechanism for directing the team mem- ber's account activity. If, for example, the objective is to have the buyer share the technical specifications of a planned plant renovation by 12/16, you can discuss this objective with the engineer who will have the discussions and then hold her accountable for realizing it on the call. As in all other cases, the call objectives should be stated in terms of *customer* not team member actions.

Allocating the Time Resources

Once objectives have been established, you can forecast the time requirements of the various team members. This is accomplished by reviewing the objectives and assigning a time limit to their completion. This time limit should be a ballpark figure based on past experiences and an average ability to accomplish the objectives. Adjustments may have to be made after the team is actually put together. In most cases, an experienced customer service rep will be able to deal with customers more effectively than a new hire. If you work with the same team all the time, much of this guesswork will be eliminated. When you have completed the plan it might look like Table 8-1.

By laying out the sales plan early and clearly you allow the team

Table 8-1

Objective Customer Agrees to:	Resource	Time	Schedule
Determine current strengths and weaknesses	Sales	3 days	1/1–1/6
Conduct time and motion study	Customer Service	10 days	1/7–1/22
Establish budgetary guidelines	Sales	6 days	1/10–1/25
Review applications software	Engineering	12 days	1/24–2/15
Define programming needs	Programmers	20 days	2/15–3/15
Define proposal parameters	Sales	5 days	3/15–3/25

members to respond and schedule their time with a minimum amount of hassle. Additionally, a hard copy tends to make the plan more set in stone and thus less subject to debate when team members are brought together.

The First Team Meeting

Once the plan has been established, it's usually a good idea to bring the entire team together. Strategies vary on what the objectives of this meeting should be. Some team sellers like to position the meeting as a "kick off" function, complete with as much fanfare and hoopla as they can muster. They feel that this generates excitement for the campaign ahead and gives the team members an opportunity to get to know each other on a more informal basis. Others take a more somber approach. They like to lay out the plan in a serious manner and let everyone on the team know that it will be a difficult struggle. Their rationale is that partying and celebrating should be reserved for when the signing actually occurs. I feel that both approaches have merit and the approach you take depends on a number of factors including:

- The nature of your team. If your read is that they would respond well to a motivational approach—use it. If not, tone it down.
- The culture of your business. Many companies frown on overly energetic meetings. If yours is one—don't buck it. It will probably backfire.
- The number of campaigns you mount in the course of a year. Fanfare may get a little old if you mount a few dozen campaigns a year.
- The schedules of your team members. You may develop some problems with their superiors if you're taking them out of the flow for long lunches or meetings.
- Your own comfort level. Many excellent salespeople don't feel comfortable with hype. This doesn't make them any less effective. Use the style that makes you most comfortable.

Regardless of how you decide to approach the meeting, be sure that you convey a personal sense of commitment and excitement over the campaign. This will transfer to the team and get you off on the right foot.

Master the Secrets of Successful Group Dynamics

It has long been recognized that people working in groups react differently than when they work alone. As group leader you can tap into these differences and maximize the effectiveness of the group effort. To accomplish this you should know how to:

- Assess the needs of each individual within your group
- Coach team members
- Influence team members even though you don't have authority over them
- Make decisions in a team setting
- Use team building techniques to refresh team spirit

Let's examine each of these points in more detail.

Assess the Needs of Each Individual Within Your Group

In Chapter 7, I discussed the need for stability in the maintenance of long-term relationships and that stability was maintained by managing change in ways that protected or enhanced power, personality, and perspective. These dynamics are at work with your sales team as well. When people enter into a team effort they have three fundamental *needs* that must be addressed in order to make them feel a part of the team:

- A need to be liked
- A need to influence
- A need to control their own roles within the group as well as the group's activities as a whole.

These needs will exist at various levels with each individual. Obviously, the new team member will have less need to control than the old veteran who has been through a hundred campaigns with you. One of the first things you should do as group leader is assess the level of need for each team member including yourself. Many team sellers use a point scale to rate these needs like this:

Influence	low	1	_____	5	high
Liked	low	1	_____	5	high
Control	low	1	_____	5	high

The purpose of this rating is to provide the group leader with a foundation for action once the sales campaign starts. Effective team leaders try to accommodate, as much as they can, the needs of each member of the group. For example, if the leader determines that one member has a strong need to influence, he might ask her a lot of questions in group meetings or assign special small group assignments to this person. If another has a strong need to control, he might be assigned with a task like keeping the minutes of meetings or designing the reporting system. By tapping into these needs, team sellers create harmony and avoid conflict. Problems occur when one or more of these needs take on such importance to the individual that it threatens the effectiveness of the team as a whole. By knowing where the problem is coming from, the team leader can more effectively deal with the conflict later on. The knowledge gained from this exercise helps the team leader choose an appropriate leadership style and develop strategies for influencing team members without actually having authority over them.

Coach Team Members

Is there a *best* style of leadership for team sellers? Yes and no. In a perfect world, the best leadership style would seem to be one that incorporates an unyielding dedication to getting the task done and a high concern for people. That is after all how most of us would want to be treated. Yet the "correct" style is often dictated more by the situation than the textbook. If your team members are relatively inexperienced, you may have to take a strong task-oriented approach until they learn the ropes. This might mean giving very specific direction on calls and presenting your sales plan in the very finest detail. On the other hand, an experienced team that has completed campaigns before may resent your interference, thus making a hands-off or low task/low personal approach more appropriate.

Only you know where your team stands currently but the high task/high personal approach will probably come into play most

often in your team selling activities and deserves more attention
here. Also known as the coaching style, it allows you to give
individual attention to team members as needed since your "public
stance" is concerned with tasks and people in equal measure.

Coaching is essentially a style that strives to let individuals
develop their own skills with little more than a helping hand from
the leader. Coaches recognize that team members have a vast
reservoir of skills and knowledge that can be tapped for maximum
benefit to the team.

Coaching is characterized by a strong respect for those skills and
knowledge and an openness to let people experiment. This description may not be consistent with your image of the great
coaches of all time. People like Bear Bryant or Woody Hayes don't
seem like the type of people who let their players experiment. Yet
if you think about coaching, the coach is in a unique position. He
can't play the games for the players. The best he can do is put
together a solid game plan, practice his players until they can
execute to the best of their abilities, and then let them do it.

Business coaching, particularly team coaching, has many paral-
lels. As much as you'd like to at times, you can't conduct all the
calls the team members must make. To a large degree, you too
have to set the game plan, perhaps practice a bit, and then let them
do it. An effective coaching style follows these guidelines:

- Describe the task to be accomplished. Establish the
  objective for the customer interaction by taking a low-
  key but firm approach: "Joe *we've* really got to get the
  procurement people to change their stress level specifications. Can you develop a testing procedure to
  demonstrate that our levels are safe?"
- Seek different approaches. Ask the other members for
  input. "How would you approach this objective?" or
  "What ideas do you have on this situation?" will get the
  flow of information started.
- Evaluate the different approaches. Lay out all the options, then determine a best course *together*.
- Get commitment to act in the way you agreed.

The coaching style creates many valuable by-products. Members feel they have "ownership" of the approach, they gain respect

for you, and they generally feel better about themselves. This goes a long way in increasing the effectiveness of the team.

Influence Team Members Even Though You Don't Have Authority Over Them

The problem of getting team members to do what you want without having the authority to impose some sort of negative consequences has taken its toll on many team sellers. It's easy to understand why this is a problem. After all, the only real role model we have for group action is the boss/subordinate relationship. This system seems to work very well. Management determines what has to be done, develops a plan of action, and monitors the performance of those who actually carry out the tasks. In order to maintain this system, your manager is empowered with the ability to impose certain positive and negative consequences on you. Among these powers are the power to evaluate your performance negatively, the power to recommend pay increases, the power to recommend you for promotion, the power to assign work, and the power to terminate your employment.

Effect of Influence
Taken in total, these powers form a powerful control over your actions and behavior. These powers don't have to be exercised in order to be effective. They exist as part of the environment in the same way that simple etiquette directs the way we behave in public. The simple fact that your manager can control, at least to some extent, your destiny, changes the relationship. If you are a sales representative that works on a straight commission with no base, you have a different relationship with your manager than a rep who works on a salary and bonus arrangement.

As team leader you don't have the same power base. In most cases, the members of your team don't even report to the same manager. Yet to be effective, the team leader has to identify some bases of power and leverage that power in order to control the activities and behaviors of the group. While the powers entrusted to the manager over subordinates reinforce *authority,* the powers the team seller develops and leverages reinforce *influence.* It's a mistake to think that influence is somehow second rate as a means of getting people to do what you want. One only need look at any

revolution to see the power of influence. In most cases, the rebels
in these situations start out with little more than an idea with which
to influence the people. The establishment has all the power of the
modern state including the ultimate authority—the power of life
and death. Yet through skillful influence, the rebels can gain
strength and support from all segments of the society until ul-
timately they gain control.

In the purest sense, **influence** can be defined as *the ability of
persons or things to get others to want to act in a prescribed way*.
The ability of a rich person to influence political figures because of
an ability to contribute to reelection is one example. The politician
is not *bound* to act in the prescribed way but he has to think twice
about taking a contrary position. Unfortunately, in many cases, this
allegiance is stronger than the allegiance the politician has to those
with authority—the voters.

Influence will usually flow naturally between you and the other
team members. Most mature adults will recognize that this is a
sales team and as the sales representative you are the logical and
appropriate leader. But for those occasional problems you may run
into, it's important to understand your bases of power and how to
leverage them.

The Team Leader's Power of Influence

The ultimate power that you as team leader possess relates
directly to the needs of the team members—the need to be liked,
the need for control, and the need to influence. By recognizing
these needs and developing strategies to leverage them, the team
seller creates a framework for control at least as strong as the
traditional manager/subordinate relationship. Let's examine some
of the powers of influence that any team leader has.

- The power of the team. This power relates to the very
  human desire not to let others down. By stating your
  pleasure or displeasure with a certain behavior, you
  can exert an enormous amount of influence. By providing positive feedback with phrases like "great job" or
  "we're really grateful" or "you're really supporting the
  effort," you create a sense of teamwork that few can
  resist. On the other hand, you can use the power of the
  team to redirect negative behavior. By using phrases

like "you're letting us down" or "I'm really disappointed," you establish a level of concern that will
often turn an individual around.

- The power of friendship. This power relates to your
  personal relationship with an individual. Since the
  team is made up of more or less equal members, the
  team leader can use friendship more effectively than a
  boss can with a subordinate. Like the power of the
  team, the power of friendship influences on a very
  personal level and can have a powerful effect in both
  positive and negative situations.
- The power to isolate. Just about every team member
  has some level of need to be a part of the team. By
  isolating a particular member for a short period you
  can convey displeasure very effectively. This can be
  accomplished by communicating only on a business
  level or by denying access to special task groups or
  assignments.
- The power of access. By denying a team member
  access to you for input and discussion you can also
  influence behavior. Of course this should not be done
  to the detriment of the team effort as a whole. You can,
  however, take a little longer getting back to an individual whose giving you a hard time.
- The power of reporting. By insisting on a different
  reporting structure for an ornery team member you
  can demonstrate displeasure. This can be done informally by asking for constant updates or formally by
  requiring written reports on all activities.
- The power of status. Like benching the superstar in
  baseball, this power relates to your ability to build up
  or deny a team member's image with other team
  members. While he's still a team member, he gets the
  message that he's not as vital to the team as he might
  have thought. This can be accomplished by calling on
  others at team meetings, by praising others while only
  mentioning the offending individual, or by physically
  distancing yourself from the individual at meetings.
- The power of assignment. This power relates to your
  power to assign or deny assignment of key tasks. This

can be used in a punishing way by requiring a team member to carry out some of the less pleasant duties of team membership or positively by assigning high-profile tasks.

- The power of the organization. The power to request a replacement for an individual is the perhaps ultimate power you possess. By requesting a replacement, you are exposing the individual to larger-scale negative consequences with her boss and the organization as a whole. It's a power that has to be used with great discretion and only when all other attempts to influence have failed.

As in the boss/subordinate relationship, these powers don't actually have to be exercised to be effective. Attempts should be made, however, to let the team members know that you possess the powers. This can be accomplished by establishing accountabilities and responsibilities early in the campaign. In your first meeting you should establish everyone's role very clearly. You should establish that you will assign tasks and set schedules and make it clear that you have the power to provide both negative and positive consequences.

The important thing to remember when trying to influence without authority is to *be discrete*. Avoid any gesture that might be construed as threatening or heavy handed. Influence is a skill that recognizes that you catch more bees with honey than vinegar.

To this point, I've been discussing ways to *prepare* yourself for group action. Now, let's move on to the *action* itself. In order to manage the team effectively, you should be aware of how decisions to act are made in groups and strategies for team building.

Make Decisions in a Team Setting

In order for you to be effective as team leader, you must get the team to take actions in a unified, cohesive way. What kind of actions? Things like:

- Presenting a unified benefits story from every team member to every customer contact.
- Standardizing fact finding activities so that all team

members are concentrating on areas that are really important to the customers.

- Withholding certain information until the timing is right.
- Being sensitive to the customer's political environment.
- Stressing one function (e.g., technical) over another (e.g., service).

If you've ever worked with a team, you know that egos, departmental perspectives, and beliefs can conspire to make unity very difficult.

One way to increase your effectiveness in this area is to understand the phases of group action.

Any group, whether it be your selling team or your local bowling team, acts in fairly predictable ways when a decision or course of action is put before them. These are called the phases of group action and generally follows these steps:

1. Orientation. In this phase, the group becomes acquainted with the tasks and requirements of the team. This phase is characterized by a lot of questions, statements, and opinions directed at clarifying and defining the task at hand.

2. Conflict. In this phase, leaders emerge, positions are established, and sides are taken. Generally, the group will develop two leaders—one concerned with the task or tasks and one with people. This conflict is not a negative thing nor is the development of leaders. Conflict is needed to ensure "buy-in" by the team members as well as to air courses of action.

3. Resolution. In this phase, the team agrees on a course of action, accepts the leadership positioning, and commits itself. This phase is characterized by extended discussion, "peacemaking," and a general lessening of tensions.

4. Reinforcement or redirection. In this phase, the group seeks to assure itself that it has made the right decision or to develop alternate courses of action. This phase is characterized by frank discussion of

what actually occurred during calls as well as seeking opinions and feedback.

Let's suppose you're the sales rep heading up a team of telecommunications experts consisting of a systems engineer or applications expert, two trainers, four installers, and a financial analyst.

You've met with the president of the account. He's a no-nonsense type of guy interested only in the bottom line. For this reason, you've decided you want to "feature" the financial analyst and let the other members go about their business without much exposure to senior management.

You anticipate that this may not go over well with the systems engineer who feels she should be the cornerstone of *every* sale. The trainers will probably not raise any objection, but the installers will be insistent that senior management know about the logistics of getting the system up. How would you go about proposing a course of action for the team?

Orientation. The key objective would be to get every member of the team customer oriented. Since you've met the president you should paint a clear picture of what he's like, what he expects, and your view of the best way to approach him. Whenever possible, quote the customer directly. This will help the team see what they're up against. When you've done that, make your recommendation: "I'm recommending that we get the finance person involved upfront and that all our meetings with customers concentrate on cost savings and efficiencies. Do you agree?"

Conflict. Look for objections from the team. If at first team members are reticent—pull it out of them. "I know we usually concentrate on applications, but in this case, I'm confident the financial approach will work better. Does the systems engineer have any problems with that?" Make sure you convey an understanding of each member's concern but don't be swayed.

Resolution. Draw the group to an agreement—even if it's a compromise. "Can we agree that finance should come with me on the next call and determine the parameters of the study?" Use the financial analyst to help reach resolution.

Reinforcement/Redirection. Once calls have been made, feedback results to the team. If possible, have the finance person explain how well it went.

The chart on the following page provides some dos and don'ts for each phase of group action.

	Do	**Don't**
Orientation	State objectives clearly	State personal preference too strongly
	Seek all opinions	Let a few members dominate
	Set a time limit	Argue
	Summarize often	Leave points hanging
Conflict	Control emotional outbursts	Allow personal attacks
	Seek many opinions	Minimize opinions or concerns
	Keep discussions on one subject at a time	Take sides
	"Playback" the essence of conflicting arguments	Impose personal biases too strongly
Resolution	"Net out" possible solutions	Allow other discussion
	Remind team members of the objectives	Allow antagonism to linger
	Establish criteria for decisions	
	Seek verbal commitments from all members	
Reinforcement or redirection	Assume a coaching style	Accuse or threaten
	Keep to the facts of the situation	Let personalities intrude
	Remain objective	Panic

If you recognize that *every* plan, change, or course of action you or another team member propose will probably have to go through these phases, you can plan for action more effectively. You can also lessen your frustration level by telling yourself that conflict and resolution are a normal part of any group action. You can even anticipate some of the actions of the group and develop ways to address problems or concerns in an efficient manner.

Use Team Building Strategies to Refresh Team Spirit

It's almost inevitable in any team selling situation that you will recognize a need to refresh the team spirit and get the team members on track. Team spirit can be damaged in a number of ways.

- Time can cause a loss of direction or enthusiasm. Often, sales that require a team approach are also sales that require long, complex sales cycles. Individual members may lose track of the initial objectives and direction of the campaign.
- Individual needs may begin to surface where they didn't before. Members may start to feel a loss of influence or control at any time during the campaign.
- Customers may negatively affect the team. Really tough customers may discourage team members who are not accustomed to some of the more unpleasant aspects of selling.
- Conflicts may develop among team members or between you and individual members.
- The original sales plan may be flawed in ways that make people second guess what they're doing.

Once you recognize that team spirit is lagging, it's vital to take corrective action as soon as possible. By ignoring it and hoping it goes away, you run the risk of allowing the problem to fester and perhaps of losing the opportunity to regain the spirit at all.

How to Recognize Why Team Spirit Is Waning

How do you go about regaining a lost or damaged team spirit? Follow these steps:

1. Identify the symptoms of the problem.
2. Determine probable causes of the problem.
3. Select and implement a team building strategy.

Symptoms can be defined as outward manifestations that something is wrong. On a sales team, symptoms may include a lack of enthusiasm at team meetings, late reports, uninspired or sloppy calls on customers, disruptive behavior at meetings, customer complaints, poor follow-up, or a host of other outward signs. As we discussed in Chapter 4, the biggest mistake anyone can make in trying to solve a problem is to attack symptoms. If you try to approach team members on issues like enthusiasm, inspired selling, or follow-up, you're probably only going to raise some resentments and damage the team spirit even further.

Instead, you have to ask yourself: "Why do these symptoms exist?" In most cases the answer to this question will come from an examination of the *needs* of the group. Are the team members feeling "unliked" because of something that you or another team member is doing? Do they feel they are losing control because of the way the sales plan is unfolding or because customers are not acting in anticipated ways? Or do they feel that they are not influencing the team's progress enough because of something you are doing at team or individual meetings? Or is it not related to the team effort at all? Are individual members having problems at home or with their boss and thereby causing the problem? The team seller can "chart" the problem before developing a strategy for building team spirit. The chart on the following page is an example of how a team seller can clearly delineate the problem.

Tested Team Building Techniques

Once the causes and possible reasons why team spirit is lagging have been analyzed, you can start to take some actions to rebuild it. There are many strategies that can be employed to build team spirit. Some are effective on a one-on-one basis while others can be used with the group as a whole. Generally, problems with influence and/or control will cause more damage than problems with the need to be liked. Because the need to control and the need to influence both relate to contributing in group decisionmaking, I'd like to focus on team building techniques that facilitate decisionmaking rather than those that enhance interpersonal re-

Table 8-2

Symptom(s)	Probable Cause(s)	Why
Joe is not contributing at meetings	Feels he's not in control	Sales call strategies have not been working
Mary has not followed up calls	Not feeling liked	I was short tempered with her after her first call
Frank's been disruptive at meetings	Feels influence is waning	We chose Joe's strategy at the last meeting and it turned out that Frank's would have worked better
Larry has not been prepared for sales calls	Feels he lacks influence	I didn't ask his opinion at the last meeting
Janice is not participating at meetings	Not sure	Not sure

lationships. While there are many more techniques, I'd like to concentrate on four that have special applications to team selling:

- Brainstorming
- Checklisting
- Task forcing
- Conflict resolution interviews

Brainstorming is a method of generating ideas with an eye toward providing a solution to a problem. Brainstorming is a free-wheeling discussion of ideas. All ideas are encouraged—no matter how strange they seem. A successful brainstorming session follows these rules:

- The problem is clearly stated. For example: "We are currently three weeks behind the sales plan. We need to develop a plan to catch up by the end of the month."
- Criticism is forbidden. Any and all ideas are encouraged and recorded equally.
- Quantity is stressed over quality. The objective is to develop as many ideas as possible.
- Combinations of ideas are encouraged.

The team leader records as many ideas as the group can come up with and then seeks to eliminate, combine, or enhance ideas until a solution becomes apparent. Brainstorming is effective in developing creativity as well as drawing out reticent members. It often falls short, however, in developing high-quality solutions unless the team leader is very skilled at conducting these sessions. Frequently, a brainstorming session will develop a number of alternate solutions that will then have to be reexamined, analyzed, and decided on. Brainstorming is probably best used when the problem is minor or where team spirit is relatively healthy.

Checklisting attempts to get to the core of a problem through development of written instruments. It can be used both to assess past team performance and to address future problems that may be anticipated. Like the checklists used in NASA's mission control, the list should be developed in ways where positive answers add up to a decision to go. A simple example might be a list of items needed to conduct an initial call on a buyer:

Appointment made?

Records reviewed?

Objectives established?

Appropriate literature gathered and organized?

Opening planned?

Objections anticipated?

Close developed?

Follow-up planned?

If the person making the call answered yes to all those questions, the decision to go ahead and make the call could be made. Checklists can be developed by the team leader or by the group as a whole. Checklisting is only appropriate when the final decision desired is a simple yes/no or go/no go decision: in other words, when there are only two possible solutions. Many team sellers use it when evaluating the entire strategy, specific objectives within the strategy, or in deciding on whether to take in new team members.

At times it's best to move some decisions away from the team as a whole and evaluate in smaller groups. This is called **task forcing** and involves selecting specific team members to attack a problem and provide a solution. Establishing a task force should follow these guidelines:

- State the problem as clearly as possible. For example: "Team cohesiveness seems to be deteriorating. This is evidenced by an increase in late reports, lack of attendance at team meetings by the programmers and customer service, and lack of follow-up on customer calls."
- Establish an objective. The task force must have its mission clearly stated. An example of a clear objective is: "Provide a strategy for returning team spirit to the level observed at the beginning of the sales campaign."
- Establish a time limit. Firm deadlines should be established and enforced so that the task force works quickly and effectively.
- Commit to the task force's findings. State clearly that you and the other team members will follow the findings and recommendations of the task force.

In most cases, you as team leader should *not* be a member of the task force. There is a possibility that you are, in fact, the cause of the problem and they should be free to examine that possibility along with all others. The membership of the task force should relate at least partially to the problem itself. If your read is that one or more members are somehow damaging team spirit, include them on the task force along with members who are still positive. This may make for a fiery task force but also may get the problem people back onboard.

The final team building strategy is the one that you will probably use most often—the **conflict resolution interview.** It is almost inevitable that conflict will arise between individual team members. An effective team seller must have the skills to air these conflicts and move to manage them before team spirit is damaged beyond repair.

These are difficult sessions. Emotions run high, defenses are up, and there is a great deal at risk. These are, of course, the *very* reasons that you must conduct the sessions. These sessions can be conducted between you and a team member or with you acting as "referee" between or among two or more conflicting members. You'll increase the effectiveness of these sessions by following these seven steps:

1. State the symptoms of the problem as you see it. This is a simple statement of concern at what you're observing. Try to state them without emotion or personal injury. A statement like "I'm concerned, Joe, that you're not participating at team meetings and I'd like to find out why" will get the job done.

2. Gain agreement to work it out. Early in the interview it's important to get a commitment that the person or persons will try to work it out. Use a simple question like "Are you willing to take a look at this problem with me?"

3. Describe the conflict. Be very specific in describing the behaviors you're witnessing, the problems the behavior is causing, and your personal feelings regarding the situation. Try to discourage dialogue at this point by starting out with a phrase like "Let me start by telling you the way I'm seeing this thing unfold. . . ."

4. Determine what's at stake. Try to probe into the areas of control or influence to determine why the person is acting this way. If that doesn't work, try looking at factors outside the team itself. Is the person having trouble with his boss? Is there a career problem? Or as a last resort are there problems at home? Encourage frank discussion and *listen* to the responses. Avoid, if you can, becoming defensive or intolerant of opposing viewpoints.

5. Determine the "family jewels." What are the areas

that the individual wishes to protect at all costs? Perhaps the person really resents interference in her workflow. Or maybe she feels a need to report and discuss activities more frequently than you're accustomed to doing.

6. Seek ways to accommodate. Negotiate a settlement based on what's been discussed. Propose ways that you might be willing to change in exchange for a renewed commitment to the team.

7. Summarize and gain a commitment. Recall all the important elements of the interview and then ask the individual to commit to a new way of doing things.

You should recognize that not every conflict can be managed in one interview. Often, you will have to meet repeatedly to discuss differences and renew commitments. By all means, however, don't give up and don't avoid these sessions. Conflict is a cancer to team selling activities. Without treatment it will eventually destroy the team. For this reason, it's important to monitor the situation and *follow up* as appropriate. Follow-up involves both raising the discussion again and again if the problem doesn't seem to be lessening *and* reinforcing an individual if he is trying to turn it around.

Keep Informed Through Reporting and Control Systems

The final consideration the team seller must contend with is controls and reporting. This is often a touchy subject with team sellers. They don't want to overmanage the team and involve themselves in areas where they don't have much expertise. On the other hand, they are accountable for the final result. Let's examine each consideration separately.

Two Types of Reporting System

Reporting systems must be established on either a formal or informal basis. Most team sellers prefer to maintain an air of informality unless problems arise. They feel that this approach is more in keeping with their role as team leader than formalized written procedures. The major reporting concern in team selling is performance against the plan. The team seller wants to know:

- Results of sales calls
- Team member decisions
- Variances from the plan

The team seller can take one of two approaches—activity reporting or exception reporting.

Activity reporting asks the team members to report, in summary form, on all activities with customers. The standard itinerary/call report that most sales organizations use is an example of an activity report. The advantages of this approach are that it keeps the team seller well informed, it encourages the team members to stick to the plan, and it allows for in-depth analysis for future planning. On the negative side, activity reporting is time consuming, difficult to enforce (how often has your boss had to hound *you* for call reports), and may cause resentments with team members.

Exception reporting asks team members to report only on variances from the plan. Generally, the variances will relate to successful or unsuccessful realization of call objectives, customer objections, or new approaches that a team member employed. The advantages of the exception reporting approach are that it is less time consuming, it highlights only the negative aspects of the plan, and it's easy to sell to team members. The disadvantages are that it relies on the integrity of the team members, it places the team seller in a reactive mode in managing the team, and it does not provide as much information for future planning.

The approach you choose should consider the following:

- The maturity level of your team. If they are experienced in team selling, an exception approach should be employed. If they are relatively new, you may wish to monitor more closely.
- The soundness of your sales plan. If you feel the plan is solid and not likely to encounter difficulties, use the exception approach. If you have doubts, ask for more stringent reporting.
- Future planning needs. If you're relatively new at planning, you may wish to have as much information as possible for future plans.
- The customer. If this is a customer who has not tradi-

tionally responded to sales efforts, you may want to maintain exhaustive records. If you determine that the customer is likely to respond well, you can lighten up.

• The dynamics of your team. If you feel that they will respond well to the activity approach and other factors also point in this direction—use it. If not, take the exception approach.

Establishing Controls

Control relates to the protocols and procedures you establish for team meetings and other communications opportunities. These controls establish how the team will operate on a day-to-day basis. The best example of one of these protocols is parliamentary procedure. In this protocol, speakers must be recognized by the "chair" and limit their remarks to a specified time frame. In most cases, this much control is not required in team selling situations. However, it's worth considering different options in light of your needs.

Essentially, there are three different approaches you can take to the issue of control. Communication can:

• Center around you
• Center around functions or expertises
• Flow freely

If you establish a protocol that states that team members must communicate through you, you increase your control over the team effort and formalize the team selling approach. You also set yourself up for a considerable amount of work and you might create some resentments. If you choose the second approach—limiting overall communication but allowing certain functions to communicate directly—you maintain control without inhibiting team spirit. In the final approach, you sacrifice some control for the sake of open communications among the team members.

In most cases, a free flow of information is desirable. You are generally going to be in the field quite a bit and not as accessible to team members as the first two approaches require. The considerations in selecting control mechanisms are very similar to those used to select reporting mechanisms.

Interacting with the Customer

The moment of truth in any team selling environment comes when your team members have to come face-to-face with the customer. Often, this interaction will take place without benefit of your watchful eye. You can drive yourself crazy if you worry too much about what happens each time a customer and a team member get together. If you find yourself "losing it," take these reality checks:

- Am I remembering that team members are *not* salespeople and are not expected to be?
- Am I trusting members to do what they promised to do?
- Am I keeping in mind that team members will be trusted for their expertise alone until they do something to lose that trust?
- Am I keeping in mind that team members are talking to peers—people with the same interests and perspectives that they have? There's a level of "salesmanship" there that any amount of selling skills will never match.

Summary

The team selling environment is an exciting and challenging way to sell. Rewards will gravitate to those that manage the effort effectively. While competitors grapple with internal problems of influence and control, a well-managed team can use its time and energies where they belong—with the customers.

9

THE PROSPECTOR

Prospecting has become a very sophisticated business in the last ten years or so. We now have highly targeted mailing strategies, focused and efficient telemarketing efforts, even interactive tape machines to do a lot of the legwork that used to be the exclusive province of the sales rep.

Yet the need for a face-to-face encounter with potential customers is still very real in the business-to-business arena. This is particularly true for situations like:

- Unbranded products like meat or cleaning products sold to restaurants and institutions. These products do not enjoy large marketing budgets designed to develop brand loyalty. Hence, switching is easy and the need for new customers is constant.
- Old and accepted technologies like certain typewriters and photocopiers. These products have developed an almost commodity status. Customers are more accepting of new suppliers since the basic mechanics are very similar.
- New channels of distribution like selling food in non-food retailers (like drug stores or mass merchandisers) or office supplies through equipment dealers. These new channels need a face-to-face encounter to have their questions and concerns answered.
- Really new ideas, products, or concepts. The truly revolutionary concept is often hard to get across in any medium other than the face-to-face call.

These factors, combined with the probability that your quota dictates that you generate volume anyway you can, make the prospector role very important to your success.

I must confess to a certain awe for those who prospect well. My own dislike for rejection and inability to maintain the high energy level that prospecting requires always inhibited me from being as good at it as I could have been. This is the first lesson I learned from effective prospectors—namely, that the greatest enemy to effective prospecting is yourself: not the market, not the competition, but your own inability to overcome fears and hang-ups.

Don't effective prospectors have fears and hang-ups? Are they somehow endowed with special personalities that make them immune to normal human weaknesses? No one, absolutely no one, likes rejection. And rejection is a fact of life in the prospector role. What makes effective prospectors different, in my view, is their ability to take rejection and a certain amount of uncertainty in stride—not because of some special personality quirk but because its part of their plan. Direct mail marketers recognize that rejection is rampant in their approach. They consider returns of 2–3% absolutely fantastic and forecast their results accordingly. Most effective prospectors feel a hit rate of 30% will make them rich. How they come to feel this way can be summed up in one word— *planning*.

Effective prospectors plan every facet of their day, week, month, and year. They know where they are going and how they are going to get there. They establish the plan and then they execute it. These planning activities can be divided into four categories:

1. Activity management
2. Territory management
3. Itinerary planning
4. Call planning

Without careful planning of these four elements, most people will become discouraged with the prospecting role and begin to find ways to avoid it.

Let's take a closer look at each of these elements.

Activity Management

Activity management recognizes that there is a *direct* correlation between the amount of calls made and the amount of sales made.

Now that may seem like an obvious point. The more calls you make, the more sales you'll get—right? But do you know how many calls, on average, it will take to make one sale? Are you aware of how many calls you can reasonably hope to make in a day, week, or month? Do you have a system for determining which accounts to call on first, second, and third and how much time to spend on each call? A well-planned activity management system allows you to answer yes to all these questions. The system contains the following components:

1. List management
2. Call to close ratios
3. Pipeline strategies

List Management

No prospector can hope to approach a market efficiently without a list or some other source material that tells her who's who. Obtaining a clean up-to-date list is always a challenge. The world changes so quickly that it's almost inevitable that certain names and locations will be obsolete before you use it. **List management** can be defined simply as the process by which you select, qualify, and use the sources of prospects.

Chances are that your organization's marketing department conducts direct marketing activities of which lists are a vital component. They probably have professionals who manage the lists and the programs. It's probably a good idea to get to know these people and how they operate. Obviously, they have far greater resources to work with than you do and they are expected to manage a list more tightly than you do. Yet fundamentally the process is very similar. Both you and marketing must try to find the best possible list for your needs. Lists can generally be placed into one of three categories:

1. **House lists** are lists kept by your own organization. They can include active customers (who may not purchase the entire product line), inactive customers, prospects who have inquired but not bought, and prospects who have been referred by existing customers. Clearly, these are the best lists for you to use since they reflect direct interest in your specific prod-

uct or service. They are also, however, probably somewhat limited in their use as a source of really new prospects.

2. **Qualified lists** are lists that other organizations keep based on responses they have received to mail or other solicitations. Obviously, the best lists would be those of *direct* competitors but these are probably going to be difficult if not impossible to obtain. So you'll probably have to get creative and start to make "connections." One successful prospector I worked with sold automated labeling devices to retail outlets. She knew that not all retailers were ready for these devices and that just to make random calls would not be profitable. She noticed that many of those who did buy also fancied electronic cash registers and inventory control devices. She got to know the salespeople for Sanyo and NCR in the area and they swapped prospects. Both sides profited with dramatically increased close to call ratios.

3. **Compiled lists** are somewhat general lists of a geographic, social, organizational, or other category of people or organizations. The most common example of this type of list (and still one of the most effective) is the yellow pages. Other examples include Chamber of Commerce lists, professional organizations, and credit rating services like Dun and Bradstreet or TRW. Compiled lists are generally comprehensive but may not be well maintained and often do not provide you with much information to qualify them.

There are so many sources of good lists that I can't begin to list them all here but Table 9-1 may give you some ideas.

Costs for these lists vary from free for many compiled lists to $100 per thousand for some very well-maintained lists. Most run from $35 to $50 per thousand. Lists can generally be broken down by zip codes and other general categories like sales or number of employees. Many can be broken down even further but that generally involves further cost. If your company does not reimburse for such expenditures (and most don't), I'd suggest making the investment yourself. A good list will pay dividends later.

Table 9-1

Type	Source
House	• Account records • District files • Marketing records • Warranty records • Customer service • Previous rep who covered the territory • Customer referrals
Qualified	• Competitive reps • Connected reps, for example, the labeling device and electronic cash registers
Compiled	• General sources* • Chamber of Commerce • Crisscross directories • Association rosters • Standard advertising directory • New businesses

*An invaluable source for lists is a publication called *Direct Mail List and Data*, published by Standard Rate and Data Service Inc., 3004 Glenview Road, Wilmette, Ill 60091.

Qualifying a list is an art that confounds even the experts. The best advice I can offer is to establish variables that are important to you. These might include sales per year, number of employees, past buying habits, years in business, or any number of other relevant facts for your business. Make the profile as comprehensive as possible by including every conceivable variable that might be of interest to you. You'll have to recognize that no list will meet all your requirements but the more comprehensive you can make it the better off you'll be. Once those variables have been established, talk to the supplier. Ask him how his list measures up to your requirements. I'd also suggest, if you have to buy a list, to purchase the smallest quantity possible (usually 1000–3000) and test it. Also, purchase the least expensive medium (printout versus labels) initially.

Working a list involves reviewing your profile of the ideal pros
pect, establishing priorities against that profile, and then allocating
time to each priority.

The more variables an account has, the higher the priority. A
helpful device to use in establishing priorities is the Juran diagram,
Figure 9-1. The Juran diagram was developed by a social scientist
to determine the relationship between sources and results. His
research showed the following results:

> 65% of results will come from 15% of sources.
>
> The next 20% will come from 20% of the sources.
>
> The final 15% will come from 65% of the sources.

You can check this against your own experience. In most cases,
65% or more of your business will come from 15% of your existing
accounts. The same can usually be said of complaints, time, and
sales calls.

This system lends itself nicely to an ABC priority system. By
looking at your list you should strive to make 15% of the accounts A
priorities based on their profile. You can assume that these
accounts will provide you with 65% of the *possible* results from that
list. The next 20% will become your B priorities based on profile
information, and the rest of the accounts will be C priorities. By
placing accounts in these categories, you establish a discipline that
will help you manage activities. It doesn't really matter whether

Figure 9-1

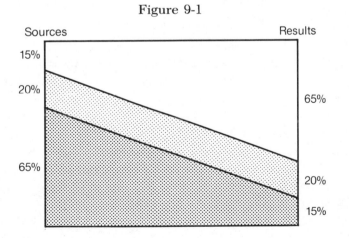

you're absolutely right in establishing these priorities—as long as you determine what you want to do first, second, and third.

Priorities tell you in what order to do things. But how much time should you spend on each priority? Most of us would say that since A priorities most closely approximate the ideal prospect that the most time should be spent there. While its true that these prospects are "easy money," to a certain extent that's just the reason they *should not* receive the most time. An account that matches your profile perfectly will usually be easier to sell. One or two calls may do the trick. A B priority, on the other hand, has some of the right characteristics but not all of them. If you were to spend, say, 80% of your time on A priorities, you would probably have great *immediate* results but what about later on? Remember that the A priorities only constitute 15% of your total list. When you've worked through them and signed your share—what then? You'll then be faced with a list of tough customers—B and C priorities. If you assume each of these prospects will require more time and effort to sell, you'll be faced with dramatically decreased sales results because you'll be forced to spend more and more time trying to close.

Effective prospectors have the discipline to invest time in long-term as well as short-term growth. They sacrifice some of the easy money for sustained sales results. I would recommend an allocation that looks something like this:

> 40% for A priority accounts
>
> 40% for B priority accounts
>
> 20% for C priority accounts

For example, if you make 40 calls per week, 16 calls should be allocated to A priority accounts, 16 to B accounts, and 8 to C accounts. As you work on C accounts a share will become B prospects. The same is true of B prospects: a share will become A prospects. By approaching the list in this way, you ensure optimum utilization and long-term results.

Once you have determined who you are going to call on, how priorities will be established, and how much of your time will be spent on the various priority levels, it's time to plan the next part of activity management.

Call to Close Ratios

Establishing realistic call to close ratios is critical to maintaining an effective prospecting plan. Its a simple process that establishes some basic assumptions about the returns you realize from sales calls. The ratio is simply what it says. The number of calls you have to make in a day, week, or month to close a sale. It requires that you be honest with yourself in terms of establishing *realistic* ratios. Obviously, this ratio will vary depending on a number of variables such as the quality of list you are working from, your own selling skills, and economic factors within your industry's marketplace. These variances are not essential, however, to establishing the basic assumptions. In most cases, the ratio will only improve as your selling skills become more refined and your ability to select lists improves. Working from a low call to close ratio is not a problem; working from a high one is disastrous.

The process for establishing a call to close ratio is simple:

1. Take a representative time frame of prospecting activities. This should be at least one week and more realistically one month. This study should take place only after you have decided on a list and completed the priority and allocation steps discussed earlier.
2. Keep track of the number of prospecting calls made during the time frame.
3. Track the number of orders you signed during the period.
4. Compare the number of calls to the number of orders. This is the call to close ratio. This ratio is usually represented like this; calls:closes.

Why is it important to establish this ratio? A ratio like this allows you to look forward by looking backward. Let's suppose you're planning your week. You determine that you can make 40 calls this week. By knowing what your call to close ratio is you can also know, with a reasonable amount of certainty, how many orders you will have at the end of the week. For example, if your ratio is 5:1 (5 calls for every 1 order), you'll know that you'll have 8 orders at the end of the week. By combining this information with your new account quota, you can determine your chances for realizing your goals.

What if you establish your ratio and compare it to your quota and determine that to realize your *monthly* quota will take at least six weeks! In other words—you don't have a chance. There are a number of steps you can take:

1. Work to improve your selling skills.
2. Increase your number of calls per week.
3. Change you list. Look for a more effective one.
4. Look for quota relief based on the *facts* of your ratio.
5. Break your priority rule and work on A prospects for awhile.

Pipeline Strategies

The final part of activity management relates to establishing pipeline strategies. What are pipeline strategies? **Pipeline strategies** relate to your in-field activities *after* you have started the prospecting effort. These are strategies similar to those an oil or gas company must employ in order to ensure a steady supply of product to consumers. Pipeline strategies determine when it's appropriate to explore, when it's appropriate to sit tight with your current supply of prospects, and when it's appropriate to move aggressively to move out prospects.

Let's suppose you have been conducting an intensive prospecting campaign for three weeks. You are working from a list with 500 accounts. During the three weeks, you were able to contact 200 accounts—leaving 300 still to be contacted.

Your efforts have been very positive. Of the 200 accounts, 100 have expressed varying levels of interest. You consider 20 to be very hot, easy money. The other 80 can go either way and will probably require more work. Your pipeline looks like this:

300 accounts not contacted

80 accounts contacted expressing varying levels of interest

20 accounts ready to buy soon

Which would you approach first? Which second? And which third? Consider what was said earlier about allocation of time: I said that the purpose of list management is to maintain as great a number of good quality prospects as possible. The same holds true once you have begun the campaign. Every account that is signed should be replaced by another qualified prospect as soon as possible. In this case, the priorities should look like this:

1. The 20 accounts ready to buy. They are ready-made sales and you need them to keep up with quota.
2. Some of the 300 accounts not yet contacted. These accounts are the raw material that will sustain your prospecting attempts. Once they are contacted, a share will become qualified prospects with a level of interest.
3. Your final priority should be those accounts that have been contacted and showed interest. Many salespeople would be tempted to return to these prospects after the hot ones have signed. If you were to do that, however, you would soon dry out the pipeline and exploration is more time consuming than selling to identified prospects.

Maintaining the Activity Management System

The system has two primary considerations that all effective prospectors recognize. One is signing as many prospects as possible within a given time frame. The other equally important and sometimes overlooked consideration is replenishing the "hopper" of identified prospects so that signing can continue. In order to ensure this orderly continuation of the system, prospectors go by the following rules:

- Establish priorities within a prospect list based on profiled variables that tend to indicate a match to their product or service.
- Allocate time at least equally between signings and replenishment.
- Create honest self-appraisals of their own abilities to close and manage their activities accordingly.

Once these components are in place, the effective prospector can maintain the system easily. In fact, maintenance as an actual activity is not really a consideration. The system maintains itself and becomes simply the way things are done.

Systematizing the management of your activities provides a number of vital benefits to the prospector:

- Because rejection is factored into the call to close ratios, the personal effect of rejection is lessened. If you've established a call to close ratio of 5:1 you know that four out of five prospects will say no (in various levels of intensity) every day. There's nothing personal about that—it's just the way it it.
- The replenishment of active prospects on an ongoing basis helps you avoid the panic of not knowing from where your next sale is coming. Because of the trade-offs inherent in the pipeline and list management strategies between long- and short-term growth, you never have to count *so* heavily on any one prospect that you become overeager and blow a sale. This improves your in-call performance as well as the overall results of your territory.
- By recognizing the system components, changes to the system can easily be made should ratios change or a given list prove disappointing.

If you believe as I do that the greatest impediments to effective prospecting are in fact your own personal weaknesses, then activity management can help to lessen that impact by forcing you to follow your self-imposed management system.

Territory Management

Territory management deals with determining where to go and how to get there. Often, salespeople lump time management and territory management together. While they do interact, territory management is not time management. Time management attempts to control and maximize the use of a resource that marches forward regardless of your attempts to maximize it. Time is a dynamic force. Certainly learning how to prioritize activities and allocate time will help you get more out of life. A territory is not nearly as dynamic a resource. It remains essentially static except for the new business activity that may take place on an ongoing basis. If your territory is the state of Iowa, it will remain the state of Iowa at least until the next revolution. Territory management strives to ensure that you are in the right place at the right time to maximize your prospecting efforts.

The elements of an effective territory management system include:

- Territory segmentation
- Itinerary planning
- Record keeping

Territory segmentation is the process by which a prospector divides her geographical territory into manageable working segments. In a pure prospecting environment, this could be accomplished fairly simply. The prospector would simply have to review the prospect list, determine the relative division of prospects, and establish more or less equal work zones to accomplish the prospecting task.

In the real world, however, there are very few pure prospecting environments. Considerations such as existing accounts that require servicing, prospect inquiries that require immediate attention, and customer decisions on where to locate facilities, all conspire to lessen the effectiveness of territory segmentation. Still, some segmentation must take place in order to direct activities most profitably. So let's take a look at some guidelines for establishing territory segments. The process should follow these steps:

1. Review the territory's geography.
2. Establish work zones.
3. Anchor each work zone with either an important existing account or a series of promising A prospects.
4. Establish priority zones based on potential.

The *territory's geography* is essential to providing effective territory segmentation. Unfortunately, there is absolutely no justice in the assignment of territories in most sales organizations. Some midtown Manhattan territories may literally be one building, while a Midwest territory in the same company may encompass two states. Variables such as quality of roads, likelihood of poor driving conditions, and urban saturation should be accounted for in taking the large view of the territory. Obviously, some areas of the territory will be more *accessible* than others, which must be a consideration when working the territory. It's often helpful to buy a number of road maps for the territory to help you start the segmentation. Well-organized prospectors complete this first phase of the segmentation by color coding various segments of the state in relation to their accessibility. They further note impediments in writing. For example: "Major road construction on route 95—will be completed in three years." By taking this macroview of the territory first, prospectors set a firm foundation for the next step in the process.

Establishing work zones is the real heart of the territory segmentation phase of territory management. Work zones are manageable portions of a territory that can be established to pinpoint prospecting activities. Work zones are established by considering the logistical elements of the territory. Ideally, a work zone can be defined as a geographical area that can be covered in an eight-hour period. Does that mean you establish a zone based on your ability to drive across it at 55 miles per hour in eight hours? Certainly not. Most territories would only have one or two work zones. Coverage has to be defined in terms of averages based on workstyle and past experiences. The factors to consider when establishing a work zone are:

- The number of calls you normally make in an eight hour day
- The average length of time each call takes
- The average time between calls

For example, if you determine that, on average, you make ten calls per day and that each call takes 20 minutes and the average time between call is also 20 minutes and you take an hour for lunch and 25 minutes for administrative duties, you can look at the territory and divide it into zones that will most probably allow you to accomplish those tasks logistically. To establish these zones effectively, you really have to be very familiar with the territory. But even if you aren't that familiar with it, you can start to establish the zones based on your geographic review.

Once the zones have been established, you should attempt to *anchor* each zone with either an existing account or a cluster of A priority prospects. This step is essential to establishing priorities in the territory. It's important to remember that not every zone will have an anchor. That's alright too. Zones that can't be anchored by either A priority prospects or existing accounts become lower priority zones in the overall territory plan. Anchors can be weighted in accordance with the concerns of the territory. If your largest account is in, say, zone 1, this will take on added weight against a zone that has only a couple of A prospects.

Once the zones have been established geographically, you can load in all the prospects you've identified in the list. This will give you a very clear picture of what's where and help to establish the priorities needed to attack the territory. Priorities are established based on *potential* to the territory. These priorities will change constantly as you make contact and start to establish business. In the early going its probably best to establish your priorities based on the largest number of A prospects. But as time goes on you'll have to consider the need for prospect replenishment as well as the demands of your existing accounts. Most prospectors find that a weekly review of the territory with an eye toward establishing priorities is enough to ensure effective coverage.

Itinerary Planning

Once the territory has been segmented you're ready to tackle *itinerary planning*. Itinerary planning is an extremely complex task. How complex? Consider this quote from *Bridges to Infinity* by Michael Guillen:

> *In the world of mathematics, too, there are problems whose large combinations of elements overwhelm our means to resolve them. Representative of this is the age-old traveling salesman problem that turns on the query, In which order should a salesman arrange cities he is supposed to visit so that he ends up traveling the least possible total distance? The answer is easy enough to fathom if only a few cities are involved, but for a large number of cities, say, fifty, there are more than* ten thousand million, million *different itineraries from which to choose.**

*Copyright 1983 by Michael Guillen. Reprinted by permission of Jeremy P. Tarcher, Inc., Los Angeles.

When taken from this perspective, itinerary planning may seem like an enormous waste of time. After all, trying to choose from 10,000,000,000,000,000,000,000 possibilities doesn't generally fit into most salespeople's schedule. Fortunately, we have a few other tricks that can make the task a little less formidable. Effective prospectors plan itineraries in the following ways:

- Reviewing the work zones
- Routing according to payoff
- Creating a plan of action

The work zone review involves simply looking at each of the work zones for opportunities to sign accounts and refill the pipeline. Following the guidelines established in the activity management section, the prospector reviews the work zones for accounts that are about to drop as well as those that have potential against the profile. Recognizing the need for replenishment, the prospector looks toward dividing his week into the 40/40/20 allocation variables stated earlier (40% on A priorities, 40% on B priorities, and 20% on C priorities). Clearly, not every zone will contain an even split of A, B, and C priority accounts. That's where routing according to payoff comes in.

Routing according to payoff is simply traveling to work zones that contain the highest number of A and B priority accounts. Generally, it's best to route yourself so that you can hit the A accounts first. Since they are likely to sign, they have the ability to prop you up for the rest of the day. If possible, C accounts should follow because they are the toughest customers and the ones where rejection is most likely. B accounts should be routed later in the day. If, however, this cannot be accomplished because of the territory, continue to route A accounts first and then follow with Bs or a combination of Bs and Cs. Routing in this way may not be the optimum method in terms of efficiency, but it does consider the human side of covering a territory. Here are some other techniques that prospectors use to organize their territories and activities:

- Start your prospecting at the closest possible point to your home or office. This helps you avoid procrastinating by making the excuses that you had to travel during "selling time." The first call of the day is always the hardest to make—so don't make it even harder.

- Use waiting time productively. Try to arrive early at appointments and ask the receptionist not to call right away. Use this time for paperwork like account records or memo writing. There are strong arguments for completing call records *immediately* after a call while the results are still fresh. Many prospectors feel, however, that this is *not* the time to do it. They often find themselves sitting in the car listening to the radio and finding ways not to make that next call. They feel that if they have some place to go its more of an impetus. So they discipline themselves to keep rolling and do the paperwork while they're at customer locations.

- Travel during lunch. One of the clearest signs that you are falling behind as a prospector is using the excuse that "no one will see me between 12 PM and 2 PM." Many unsuccessful prospectors use that as an excuse to exercise their taste buds at Denny's. Lunch is the perfect time to work yourself across town or travel to that out of the way location in the suburbs. You sacrifice the pleasures of the soup and sandwich special but you may be able to make up for it with a French meal with the commissions you make.

- Keep a clipboard with a pen attached by string or rubber bands beside you at all times. Note new construction or new businesses as you drive. No list will be as up-to-date as your own observations. By jotting down new prospects you're carrying out one of the fundamentals of activity management—prospect replenishment.

- Always make one more call than you planned. One prospector I knew kept track of his call to close ratio on end of day calls to see how they measured up against the territory as a whole. To his amazement his hit rate was three times greater on these calls over a period of three months. "There's something about pushing yourself that extra yard," he said. "It seems to surprise prospects to see a salesman at 4 PM. They almost always see you and surprisingly they're generally very attentive."

- Use music to psyche yourself up. One prospector I know used to choose her tapes very carefully at the beginning of the week. She played soft ballads in the early morning on her way to the work zone and progressively picked up the beat as the day went on. "Michael Jackson's 'Beat It' is the perfect remedy for the 2 PM blahs," she said.
- Get to know your own rhythms. I believe that there are morning people and night people, that some of us get the motor started sooner than others. Try to plan your toughest prospects when you're at your best.
- Organize your car like an office. Keep literature and other materials efficiently filed in boxes in the trunk. Tab the files for quick reference and place the most used pieces in the front. This prevents ruining your suit while you fumble around during rainstorms.
- Take stock of your performance twice a day. New York's Mayor Koch is fond of asking his constituents "How am I doin' " from time to time. It's a good idea for you to do the same. About 11 AM and 3 PM are good times to take a few minutes to assess your call to close ratio for the day and review your daily plan. If you're on target you'll feel great and move through the rest of the day effortlessly. If you're off target you can rededicate yourself and get back on the stick.
- Check for messages only during lunch and at the end of the day (about 4:30 PM). This will prevent distractions and keep your attention on the prospecting activities.

Appointments or Not?

The debate rages among prospectors over the value of making appointments. On the one hand, appointments cut down on waiting time and prevent long trips that end in a meeting with a receptionist. On the other hand, making appointments take a great deal of time themselves and many prospectors find they can't use the telephone to convey their messages as effectively. The answer for you depends to a large extent on the nature of your business. Some prospectors conduct business in markets that never require appointments. Small retailers for example wouldn't be sure they *could* even keep an appointment. Others deal in markets that absolutely require an appointment before they'd consider seeing salespeople. The answer seems to be a compromise of the two extremes. Certainly having a few appointments sprinkled throughout the day keeps you on track. If you know you have an appointment on the west side at 11 AM, you can start to work yourself in that direction early in the morning. Most prospectors seem to establish three firm appointments during the day and make the rest of their calls without them. They establish a maximum time they will wait for a prospect and if they haven't met by that time they ask if they can make an appointment at a future date.

The Telephone, the Mail, and the Blitz

No discussion of prospecting would be complete without a consideration of three of the other techniques available to the prospector—the phone, the mail, and the blitz.

As I have said earlier, the telephone has had a major effect on the way we sell and distribute goods and services. In many organizations, it has virtually replaced prospecting as a sales representative activity. The telephone clearly offers many benefits to the prospector:

- It's efficient. A morning of well-planned telemarketing can probably cover as many prospects as a week of field canvassing.
- It's cost effective.
- It's somewhat impersonal. By that I mean if there is rejection it doesn't sting quite as badly as a face-to-face meeting.

Most prospectors use the telephone for lead generation, qualifying, and appointment setting rather than for actual selling. When used for these purposes, it's absolutely without competition. To use the telephone effectively follow these steps:

1. Establish a call objective.
2. Outline the dialogue.
3. Plan the close.

I've written at great length on the need to determine a desired customer action *prior* to beginning sales calls. The same is true with the telephone. If you are using the telephone to qualify, state the objective in terms of the answers you wish to hear. For example: "The prospect will reveal her current supplier, monthly volumes, and current price levels." It's best to cluster calls around a single objective. For example, it's better to make 30 qualifying calls than 10 qualifying, 10 lead generators, and 10 appointment calls. By clustering you set your mind on that objective and improve your effectiveness.

There are two accepted approaches to planning the dialogue in telemarketing—scripting and outlining. Scripting is a method by which the telemarketer essentially memorizes a dialogue and repeats it as often as possible in the course of a day. Outlining lets the telemarketer "freelance" a little by adding his own words to an outline of key points and questions. Most experts agree that the outline approach is more appropriate for the business-to-business environment because of the sophistication of the buyers and the complexity of the sale. Outlining the dialogue consists of preparing an opening, listing some pertinent questions, and planning benefits.

The major difference between telemarketing and face-to-face selling is the customer's attention span. If you are standing in front of someone and maintaining eye contact, they are more likely to give you their attention. The telephone call, on the other hand, may have interrupted them from their most important activity of the day. They can't see you so they can't make much of a judgment on the value of communicating with you. Chances are their judgment will not be favorable. Because of this, the opening moments of the telemarketing call are essential to the overall success of the effort.

The opening should be short and to the point and contain some point of interest for the prospect. You should also identify yourself and the company immediately. Here are some techniques:

- The special offer. This technique can be used with or without a *real* special offer. It's appropriate for appointment setting, lead generation, and qualifying. It goes something like this: "Mr. Jones, Hank Phelan from Amalgamated Chocolates. We're currently offering a spcial promotion on our chocolate madness line to qualified retailers that I'd like to tell you about. How would you feel about answering a few questions?"

- The survey. This technique positions the prospector as a researcher and attempts to elicit information. It's particularly appropriate for qualifying. Here's an example. "Mr. Smith, I'm Mary Tonelli from Hirsch Business Forms. We're conducting a survey of data processing managers in the Boston area and wondered if you'd have any objections to answering ten short questions."
- The pitch. In this technique the prospector makes the offer early in the call and solicits reactions. It's appropriate for appointment setting and lead generation but may cause problems with unqualified accounts. It goes something like this: "Mr. Johnson, this is Ralph James from Computer Mania. We've recently developed a promotional package that includes a dual drive Model 6700 PC with monochrome screen, Itchygoomy graphics printer, and three software packages for $1700. How does a package like that measure up to your current pricing for similar systems?"
- The "keep up with the Joneses." In this technique the prospector uses his knowledge of the immediate neighborhood to create a sense of urgency with the prospect. It's appropriate for appointment setting. An example might be: "Ms. Frazier, this is Oscar Fromme from American Cash Register. We've recently sold our model 800 electronic cash register at Marinos Stationery, Maury's Tavern, and Bea's Dresses. While in the area I noticed your store didn't have a modern system. I wondered if I could ask you a few questions with an eye toward setting up an appointment?"
- The easy yes series (or its cousin the easy no series). In this technique the prospector moves quickly into a series of questions designed to get the prospect thinking. It's appropriate for lead generation, appointment setting, and qualifying. It follows a pattern something like this: "Ms. Davidson, this is Frank Ward from International Gear. Are you familiar with our product? Do you currently have needs for replacement gears in your automated machinery? Are you concerned with quality in these gears? And are you concerned with

getting the best price for these gears? International has just launched a new line of high-efficiency, low-cost gears that I think could be helpful to your operation. Would an appointment next Thursday at 10 AM be appropriate?"

Of course there's nothing to prevent you from using the other opening techniques discussed in this book—the general benefit statement, the question, or the case history/referral. The important thing to remember is to search for points of interest and then present quickly and compactly.

Your questions should also be planned as quick, easy-to-answer affairs that will spark some interest without requiring a lot of time. They should relate directly to your call objective. It's usually best to start with a few closed end questions (questions that can be answered yes or no or with short answers) then move on to a few open questions, and close with a closed end question. If you've kept your objective simple and attainable, your questions shouldn't have to be too complex. Use them to gather essential background information for your face-to-face call, then go for your close.

The close should be a simple call for action, stated as a question just like any other call. "Can we agree on an appointment for Friday at 1 PM?" "Can I send you literature on the 4300 and follow up with you next week?" "You're currently handling 15,000 orders a month at a price of 0.05 cents per transaction—is that correct?" These are all examples of effective closes.

The mail also provides the prospector with an avenue of communication. Your marketing department can start a dialogue through reply cards and 800 numbers in their direct mail campaigns. While your ability to start a dialogue is more limited, it's not impossible. Most prospectors include return phone numbers and addresses in all correspondence and some even include applications and order forms. Mail is not, however, a primary means of actually signing business in most situations. Instead, the prospector uses the mail to pave the way for personal or telephone contacts. This is usually accomplished by mailing to a select number of prospects in a work zone relating some offer or benefit and stipulating a follow-up activity on your part. Here are some guidelines you should follow when creating prospecting letters:

- Create a specific offer. The offer may include information, special pricing, delivery or service options, or anything else relating to your product. This is the central theme of your letter and should be included in your opening and of course in the offering.
- Remember to whom you are writing. Keep in mind that this is a letter not a speech. Keep it simple and stay with the facts. Avoid technical language, philosophy, multisyllable words, and humor.
- Prove your claims and statements. Use actual examples of cost savings, efficiencies, or other claims.
- Make the letter just long enough to get your message across—not longer.
- Ask the prospect to do something. Call, write, accept your call, or agree to an appointment are all appropriate actions for a customer to take.

The number of letters you send should not exceed the number of telephone calls you can make in a morning. This is important so that you avoid getting too backed up with prospects for follow-up. You should try to follow up within ten days of your mailing date so that the message remains fresh with the prospect. Your follow-up call should allude to the letter, refresh the prospect's memory, and then follow the telephone guidelines discussed earlier.

You should attempt to keep records of your mail and telephone campaigns to determine if certain types of prospects respond to these approaches better than others. Your record should include the type of business the prospect is in, the level of decisionmaker, the prospect priority (A, B, or C), volume, current supplier, and any other information you deem valuable. Figure 9-2 presents a form that can serve as a starting point. By reviewing the record periodically you may be able to develop a trend that says competitor X is more vulnerable than Y or that office managers respond to letters more often than purchasing agents.

The blitz is the final prospecting technique I'd like to consider. The blitz has some of the same objectives as the telephone and mailing techniques. It's used to approach the greatest number of prospects in the least amount of time. Instead of using phone or

Figure 9-2

Prospect	Priority	Type	Decision Maker	Competition	Volume

mail power, however, it uses foot power. The blitz works something like this. The prospector approaches as many prospects as
possible in a given time frame. Usually, they develop or use
existing written material as a "leave behind" with customers. They
simply enter the office, ask for the name of the person that might
handle their business, leave the literature behind, and move on to
the next prospect. They then follow up either in person or by
phone the next day. They can generally cover from four to five
times as many prospects using this method as a traditional prospecting method. Often a number of reps will blitz one territory a
week, thereby increasing the number of prospects contacted. The
blitz is especially appropriate if you have a limited time offer, work
a highly concentrated area (such as a downtown territory), or are
introducing yourself to the territory. Your call to close ratio will
probably decline in this situation simply because of the number of
calls you'll be making. This should be more than countered,
however, by the *actual* number of signings you achieve.

Call Planning

The final planning activity that the prospector must approach is
call planning. It's not very valuable to spend all that time ensuring
that you're in the right place at the right time if, once you get
there, you don't know how to handle yourself.

One of the interesting things about prospecting calls is how very
similar they can be, particularly first calls. If you think back on
your own experience, I think you'll notice that there are probably
more "surprises" from your existing accounts—those you thought
you knew—than your new prospects. They may appear at first to
be another one of those paradoxes of sales. But is it really? Here
you are—a stranger—approaching me for the first time with a
business proposition. What are my reactions going to be? Generally, I'm going to be a bit wary if not downright defensive. Probably
the best you can hope for on a first-time prospecting call is indifference.

While this is not a wonderful situation, it does have a bright side.
It allows you to *plan* a call with a reasonable certainty of success.
Those customers you know become as unpredictable as any human
being. But those thrust into the prospecting situation will generally
react in somewhat predictable fashion. Planning for those predict-

able behaviors is the final difference between successful and unsuccessful prospectors. The prospecting call plan contains the
following elements:

- An opening
- Qualifying questions
- Benefits story
- Trial close
- Discussion

Unlike the consultative seller, the prospector must sell from a
basic assumption that the prospect is ready to buy. And while there
may be elements of the negotiator role (especially in the discussion
phase of the call), in reality the prospector is *looking* for objections
and attempting to handle them. The prospector must take this
approach for one simple reason—time. If the prospector were to
take the time needed to negotiate or consult successfully, she
would probably be bodily removed from the premises or at least
severely set back in her territory plan. This is not to say that the
prospector is a "hit and run" artist but rather that the nature of her
product or service is one that requires quick decisions by the
prospect. Let's look at each element of the call plan in more detail.

The Opening

Here we go again with another statement of the importance
of the first few seconds of a sales call. Sorry for the redundancy
but . . . In the prospector role the opening is all. If you've ever
prospected I'm sure you've been through that ultimate of humilia-
tions—you know, the one where you introduce yourself, smile,
and feel your stomach sink as the prospect turns and walks away.
Thankfully, rudeness does not pervade American business as totally as some would have us believe. Still, the need to gain attention
and generate interest is vital to a successful prospecting call. The
opening flows through three phases:

- A statement or question to gain attention
- An assessment of the prospect's response
- A statement or question to generate interest

The statement or question that gains attention is designed to take the prospect's mind off whatever he was thinking before you entered and focus that attention on business issues. You can't assume that because you walk into an office or store that the world is just going to go away. Think about meetings you have with your own boss. Does she always give you her undivided attention, *every time* you enter the office? So when planning your first few opening lines keep that focus in mind. Here are a few techniques that successful prospectors use:

- The simple inquiry. This is a *very* simple question that asks the prospect to comment on some aspect of his operation. For example: "I was noticing your end aisle display in aisle 3—is that mylar?" The simple inquiry gets the prospect to focus on a business issue—however simple.
- The compliment. The compliment should be directed toward the prospect's *operation* not the prospect himself. For example: "Your factory floor seems to be one of the most organized I've seen." Avoid being too flowery in your praise so that suspicion isn't raised.
- The straight introduction. Often, your company will gain the customer's attention. By handing her your card and introducing yourself you may gain the attention you seek. This approach is particularly appropriate if you have a product or service in very high demand.
- The shock treatment. This is the opposite of the compliment—almost. While it's not a derogatory statement, it is meant to shake up the prospect. It might go something like this: "While waiting in the reception area I was noticing some of your employment applications. Are you sure you've got the best designed form for that purpose?" The shock treatment is risky. Your tone of voice should be pleasant and you should smile while delivering it. But for the right prospect it will have the desired effect.
- The referral. The referral is used when you have been "bucked" to a prospect by someone higher in the organization. It should include some statement of interest by the "higher up" such as: "Mr. Phelps I'm

- Nancy Rand from Galvanized Aluminum. I was just
  speaking with Mr. Tyson in procurement and he expressed interest in our siding products. He suggested I
  talk to you about possible applications."

Of course, there's nothing to stop you from using some of the
techniques discussed in the telephone section of this chapter. The
survey, "keep up with the Joneses," and special offer techniques
may all have applications in gaining attention.

Of the three phases of the opening, the one most ignored by
prospectors is assessing the prospect's response. This may be due
to nervousness or a lack of confidence but too often we shoot right
into the interest phase without seeing where we stand with the
prospect. This is unfortunate because it's virtually impossible to
generate interest when you haven't gained attention. By taking a
few moments to assess the reaction, you can instantly adjust to
generate maximum interest. Essentially, prospect reactions can be
placed into one of four categories:

- Attention—where the prospect displays attention and
  a willingness to listen.
- Friendliness—where the prospect displays a friendly
  demeanor but not necessarily one of attention. This is
  perhaps the most dangerous to the prospector because
  you can't really be sure whether or not he's with you.
  Some of the friendliest prospects have no more inten-
  tion of buying than the most hostile.
- Indifference—where the prospect does not display
  attention.
- Hostility—where the prospect displays outward annoyance with you.

Of the four, friendliness and indifference are the most difficult to
handle. For each reaction, however, there are specific interest-
generating strategies that will maximize your effectiveness.

Interest is defined as the prospect's desire to listen to the terms
of a proposition or proposal. It's very difficult to sell anything
without first ensuring that you have the prospect's interest. Here
are some strategies for generating interest:

- Questions. A well-stated question that forces the prospect to reflect will often generate some interest. Examples might be "Mr. Thomas are you absolutely certain you are receiving the best service?" or "Ms. Grand do you have *any* doubts about your current supplier?"
- Benefits. A well-placed statement of what's in it for the prospect may also generate interest. These benefits should relate to cost savings, operating efficiencies, or other "hot" items.
- Case histories. Like those discussed in Chapter 4, these case histories should be short demonstrations of benefits you were able to realize with other customers.
- Challenges. These are short phrases that challenge the prospect to review her operation with an eye toward closer examination. For example: "Most production managers I've spoken with find a need to continually reexamine their technology commitments."

Certain strategies work better with certain prospect reactions. To the prospect exhibiting attention, any of the strategies would be appropriate. This prospect is after all exhibiting a willingness to listen and participate. Whatever strategy you're most comfortable with will probably work best. The friendly prospect is more of a problem. He *seems* ready to listen but you're not quite sure. In this case, it might be best to employ the question or challenge strategy to see exactly where you stand since these strategies *require* a reaction. The indifferent reaction also has elements of the unknown about it. While it may *appear* that the prospect is not interested, you can't really be sure. The question and challenge strategies work well with this reaction. The case history also works well as long as you follow it with a question like, "Would you be interested in realizing similar savings?" In the hostile reaction, you're trying to calm the prospect down. This can best be accomplished by getting her to reflect on her operation. The challenge and the question strategies work very well with hostile buyers as long as they are the *right* challenge or question. Table 9-2 can help you make the decision on which strategy to use.

There are, of course, no guarantees that any of these strategies will have the desired effect on *every* call. But by planning your

Table 9-2

	Question	Benefit	Case	Challenge
Attention	✓	✓	✓	✓
Friendliness	✓			✓
Indifference	✓			✓
Hostility	✓			✓

opening ahead of time, you increase the probability that you will manage the call the way you desire.

Qualifying Questions

Once you have ascertained that attention has been gained and interest generated, you can move to qualifying the prospect. Many prospectors find this to be a difficult part of the call. They feel uncomfortable asking a prospect whether or not he has the resources to do business. Many ignore this step altogether and move right into defining needs or presenting benefits, risking embarrassment for the prospect and wasting time for themselves. A well-planned qualifying step can avoid much of this strain. In most cases qualifying involves:

- Determining the areas you want to qualify. In most cases these areas will include one or more of the following:
  — Financial resources
  — Willingness to make a change
  — Authority
  — Knowledge
  — Personal security
- Designing questions that will *indirectly* garner the information.

It would be great if you could just walk into a prospect's office, ask him if he has any money, and pitch him on your product. That may be an effective way of determining who *isn't* qualified, but it may cause some problems with those who are. By drawing on your knowledge of the marketplace, you can develop questions that will bring out the needed information without offending or embarrassing anyone. What the questions are, will, to a certain extent, depend on your business. However, there are some more or less standard questions that many effective prospectors use to qualify prospects. Table 9-3 can help you develop your own. These are only a few examples of the sort of nonthreatening questions you can plan for a prospecting call.

Benefits Story

Once the prospect has been adequately qualified, most prospectors begin an explanation of what they have to offer. This may seem

Table 9-3

Qualifying Area	Questions
Financial resources	• What is your normal per unit cost? • Is this a line item on the budget? • Can you tell me your budget for this item? • What would you estimate your expenditures are for this item?
Willingness to change	• How often do you review suppliers? • How long has it been since you've made a change? • What factors would make you contemplate a change?
Authority	• Does a purchase like this come from your budget? • Who besides you is involved in a decision on this product? • If we were to come to an agreement, would you sign the order?

Table 9-3 *(continued)*

Qualifying Area	Questions
Knowledge	• Are you familiar with word processing programs? • What has been your experience with word processors? • Have you seen word processors demonstrated?
Personal security	• Have you been in this position long? • Have you made purchases like this before? • Do you feel making a change at this time would be risky?

to contradict what was stated in Chapters 4 and 5. In those chapters, I said that it was important to explore needs and interests with the buyer before telling the benefit story. Because of the nature of the prospecting sale, however, you can't be sure that interest will be maintained long enough to complete such an exploration. Instead, the prospector looks to communicate the benefits and seek reactions. I don't think it's necessary to review the skill of selling benefits other than to say that it involves not just describing the product or service but also telling the customer what's in it for her.

Trial Close

When the benefit story has been told it's time to solicit reactions. One of the most effective ways to accomplish this is the trial close. The trial close is a question that asks for a reaction without necessarily asking for the business. Trial closes can be used to determine attitudes, gather more information, move the prospect closer to a final close, further qualify the prospect, or open up new avenues of needs or interests. There are probably as many trial closing techniques as there are ways to phrase a question. Formulating the one that's right for you is determined by what you want to accomplish. Some techniques that have proved successful are the following:

- The "What if   " close. This trial close asks the prospect to speculate on how it would be to do business. An example might be: "What if we were to deliver an initial order of two dozen. In what area of the plant would you use them?"
- The assumptive close. This trial close takes an assumptive approach by asking questions such as: "When you order would you prefer itemized invoices or bulk billings?"
- The choice close. In this trial close the prospector provides two alternative courses of action. For example: "Would Thursday deliveries be OK, or do you prefer Tuesdays?"
- The "touchy feely" close. This trial close is a direct question of attitudes and feelings. "How would you feel about doing business with another vendor after all these years?" is an example of this type of close.
- The "what else" close. This close tries to move the prospect forward by asking her "what else?" An example might be: "What else do you need to know before we sign the agreement?"

Trial closes can be thought of as probes in the prospecting sales call. They can be used repeatedly during the call to move the prospect closer and closer to final agreement. They do, in effect, raise objections and concerns. That, of course, is what the prospector wants and is generally the subject of the discussion phase.

Discussion

The discussion phase of the prospecting call attempts to air all differences, handle all objections, and close the sale. Because the discussion phase is generally set up by the customer's reaction to the trial close, the prospector is in the driver's seat. He can sit back and let the customer vent her concerns and objections, then carefully plan a response. Most prospect objections fall into one of three categories:

- Indifference. The customer really isn't interested in what you're selling or hasn't been paying attention to what you've said.

- Misunderstanding. The customer doesn't understand your offer.
- Conflict. What you are proposing conflicts with the way things are done now.

All three types of objections are really a request for further information. In most cases, the buyer is not saying "I don't want to do business with you—so get out of my office." Instead, they are saying "I don't want to do business as you proposed but let's continue to talk." I know I said earlier that objections are "handled" in the discussion phase and I'm not sure that's a correct use of words. I'm not convinced that objections are ever really "handled." Instead, they are examined, discussed, and a decision is made over whether or not it's really important enough to end the dialogue. In many cases, it will be and no techniques are going to change that. But if you approach an objection rationally and calmly, you'll be surprised at how often the positive determination is made. In order to do that, follow these guidelines:

- Acknowledge the objection. Recognize that the prospect has the right to object and that this objection is not the ranting of some off-the-wall lunatic. Phrases like "A lot of people ask that question" are effective here.
- Repeat the objection. Using your own words, try to isolate the objection to its most narrow focus. For example, if the objection is price, determine whether its unit price, discount level, or quantity price.
- Solicit the prospect's agreement that this is, in fact, the objection. After you have repeated the objection be sure to clarify it with the prospect.
- Provide clarification or counterbalancing benefits. If the objection is based on misunderstanding, you may only need to clarify. If the objection is based on indifference or conflict, you'll probably have to do more selling. As you offer the counterbalancing benefits, use trial closes to assess attitudes. Use phrases like "Do you agree . . .?" or "Does that sound reasonable to you . . .?" These will ensure the continued involvement of

the prospect and soften any antagonism that may be
building.
- Attempt a close. Once you are satisfied that you have
  aired and discussed the objection adequately, try again
  for a commitment.

By carefully planning calls, prospectors can improve both their
call to close ratios *and* their overall efficiency in the territory. By
knowing where they are going in a call they can keep one step
ahead of the prospect and maintain their own positive attitude.

Summary

While the role of the prospector may be in decline in many
industries across the country, the essential skills of keeping yourself up and organizing your activities can be translated to any of the
other five roles. Nothing, in my view, will more sharpen your skills
for selling in the other roles than a periodic foray into prospecting.
For the small-growth companies that are the backbone of this
country, the prospector will continue to provide the means for
growth and expansion. Of all the roles I've discussed in this book,
none requires greater skill and—yes—real courage than the prospector.

Index